ASCENDING NAMESAKE MOUNTAIN

Road Trips into a Wilderness

David A. McGuire

Ascending Namesake Mountain
Road Trips into a Wilderness
Author: David A. McGuire
Editors: RaeAnne Marie Scargall, Griffin Mill
Cover Design & Interior Layout: Michael Nicloy

All photographs and maps © David A. McGuire

Ascending Namesake Mountain
Road Trips into a Wilderness

ISBN: 978-1-945907-30-2

Published by Nico 11 Publishing & Design
Quantity order requests can be emailed to:
mike@nico11publishing.com

Be well read.

www.nico11publishing.com

In Memory of:
David Koenig
and
Kenneth Rowe

Ascending Namesake Mountain

PROLOGUE

This narrative account is written from the perspective of the biological, yet non-custodial, parent of his children. Data sourced from a number of publications over the years reveal statistical trends indicating *"that fewer than half of all children born today—and perhaps as few as one quarter—will live their lives with both of their parents throughout childhood."*[1]

There are millions of biological parents navigating a non-custodial boat in family life. It is a small boat, often with little space available for more than one. Watercraft such as these are subject to difficulties amplified, singular loneliness, and are vulnerable to the high risk of floundering in stormy seas. I owned such a boat. The boat leaked, didn't steer well with others, and tended to being engulfed by fog. Relationships became obscured, went adrift, and one, most precious, had been lost to locations unknown. I was a two-time loser, having twice lost at love, and the family created in each attempt. My imperative was to at least keep within sight of my second child, and stay meaningfully engaged.

With my son, a steady relationship had been possible to be maintained, though on a disjointed and irregular basis. There had been many crosscurrents of doubt, tumult, and distance, with few highs to balance the emotional lows of the first few years. As a teen, Justin's time together with me grew more frequent, dynamic, and more validating. By the time of our planned road trip vacation, we were even working together. His first job was at my own place of employment, and for that past year it was a simple and gratifying pleasure to see and be with him multiple evenings every month. I had become something more than a part-time parent. We had grown into a partnership, of sorts. My boat now appeared to be sailing as designed, in the clear, and *with* the current instead of against it.

1 Meyer David D.

Adventure is usually defined as an exciting or very unusual experience. It is characterized as a bold, risky undertaking that often involves hazardous action and an uncertain outcome. Associated terms such as fortune, luck, danger, and peril typically lend sizzle and human attraction to pursuits of adventure. For some reason, few can resist.

The telling and listening to tales about adventure must certainly be at the very core of humankind. The 41,000-year-old El Castillo Stone Age cave paintings of Spain tell a story. From ancient folklore myths and fables orally retold, to the earliest writings of and by ancient civilizations, stories of adventure are spoken of, written, embellished, and emulated to this day.

Though many accounts about mountains and excursions exist, my personal one seemed unique.

A mountain is defined as a landmass that projects conspicuously above its surroundings and is bigger than a hill. Ancient cultures would often describe this topographical edifice as a doorstep to the home of the gods in the heavens. A peak of a mountain is, after all, at that point of earth closest to them, and consequently were very often considered sacred. Quite rare it was that people of the past would climb mountains and dare trespass the realm of the deities; taboo even.

Reverence is clearly noted in the major religions' sacred texts. The Hebrew Bible mentions more than twenty different mountains, including Noah's Mountains of Ararat, Mount Zion of Jerusalem, and of course, Mount Sinai. The Greeks' Mount Olympus, the Muslims' Sulayman Mountain, Mere Mountain of Hinduism, and the Sacred Mount Fuji of Japan are vivid examples attesting to humankind's superstitions, fascinations, and awe of these massive geological formations of the earth. And yet, only recently in Western Culture have mountains represented anything much more. Rather, mountains were something mostly thought of as unproductive, to be avoided, and considered an impediment to the spread of civilization.

The first recorded climb of a mountain in the British Colonies of America was by a guy named Darby Field. Living in what is now the State of New Hampshire, this thirty-two year old Englishman of Irish descent climbed a mountain he called the "White Hill." On an overcast spring day in 1642, Field convinced one or two members of the local Abenaki tribe to accompany him up the

Saco River, to the base of what the Indians called "Agiocochook." Once there, the Native Americans refused to continue, fearing evil consequences. Alone, our hero mountaineer proceeded to climb the eminence. At 6,288 feet of elevation, it is the tallest mountain in New England, and is now known as Mount Washington. There is no first hand written account of why he did so. No purpose is known to have been mentioned. Field's contemporaries just said Darby was a harmless eccentric.

Reports of Darby's strange deed was talked about by people of the time, and even John Winthrop, the Governor of the Massachusetts Bay Colony, had heard of it. He thought it a behavior most strange. Almost no one climbed mountains in the 17th Century. When Darby Field died in 1649, it was said that his life was of "merriness, marred by insanity."[2] Insane or lucid, he would receive justice of sorts. His story survives as chapter one of American mountaineering.

My story is about a Father-Son road trip vacation to the Northern Rocky Mountains. The intention was to photograph a mountain with our name on it. Due to the calamities, obstacles, and moving goals that occurred, the short story… errrr… grew longer, with unforeseen adventures.

2 Isserman

CHAPTER
ONE

Spring, 1996

"How would you like to see a mountain with your name on it?"

Justin looked up from across the table as if startled. The bright lights of the late-night diner cast aside all shadows and deep preoccupations with the remains of his hash-browns, eggs, and toast. Eyes widening and pupils growing, a quizzical expression formed on his face as he focused at me with full attention. Then the eyelids narrowed a bit, his mind studying for a moment possible implications of such a question.

As an impish grin and small involuntary chuckle emerged, he inquired, "Where is it?" His eyes began sparkling and dancing with anticipation.

"It's in a National Wilderness Area not far from Yellowstone," I answered.

My own smile betrayed a now shared sense of excitement. The realization that my task of enrolling this sometimes detached and reluctant fifteen-year-old to this new brainstorm of mine was unfolding better than I'd hoped.

Choosing my next words carefully, I continued, "The area is in the Northern Rocky Mountains…in Idaho. There are no roads, no motorized vehicles are allowed; just hiking by foot or hoof, and tent camping with minimal amenities. The area is more primitive and undisturbed than the parks. It has many well-defined trails, though. Maybe we could hike in close enough to climb it, or at least get a picture or two. We could maybe camp out a couple of nights there. Do you think you'd like to do that?"

"I didn't know there was a mountain with our name on it. How big is it?" my son asked with wonder.

"I didn't either, but it's big, over 10,000 feet. It's designated as Mount McGuire on a map that I located it on, so it's likely to be one of the taller mountains within the Wilderness Area." Hoping that these words had contained the next stitches to sew up his affirmative I followed with, "What do you think?"

"Yeah! Heck yeah!" he exclaimed immediately, a huge smile breaking out.

This short conversation began our endeavor known as "The Father-Son Road Trip," an American rite-of-passage of sorts for both father and son. In retrospect, it was that and more—a clear line-of-demarcation in our lives. A summer vacation to view the awesome national geography we'd seen only on film would become tangible. History on printed page would come alive. The physical and personal obstacles, challenges, and achievements would transform us. New and very exciting objectives and goals would be seeded. Real and life-guiding insight and accomplishment would occur. This destination would ultimately become an obsession for me. What we found there and what was revealed in the years that followed produced questions and mysteries that still defy explanation even today.

"Road Trip" is generally defined as a journey taken on roads by automobile, typically over a great distance. The first successful North American road trip was accomplished in 1903 by H. Nelson Jackson, Sewall K. Crocker, and a dog named Bud. They drove a Winton Touring Car produced that same year, dubbed "Vermont,"[3] to journey sixty-three days between San Francisco and New York. The cost was $8,000 (about $85,000 in modern currency), which included the gas, food, lodging, tires, parts, other supplies, and the vehicle itself. Not including my own fully depreciated car, I expected to spend about $2,000 for a planned seventeen days with gas, food, lodging, camping equipment, fees, and souvenirs. Road trips are a much better deal now.

The Frank Church "River of No Return" Wilderness is a protected wilderness area in central Idaho. Created in 1980 by the U.S. Congress, it is now the second largest wilderness in the lower forty-eight states. It consists of 2.367 million acres of mountain ranges, extensive wildlife, and coniferous forests. Split by the grand valleys of the Main Salmon River and its tributary river, the Middle Fork Salmon, as the crow flies, the area is approximately one hundred miles wide, east to west, and 150 miles, north to south.

The size of this wilderness provides secluded habitat for a

3 https://www.history.com/news/the-first-great-american-road-trip

wide variety of mammal species, including some that are rare and vulnerable. This protected wilderness is the core of over 3.3 million acres of primitive and road-less area. Sizable populations of mountain lions, gray wolves, lynx, coyote, black bears, and red fox predators exist in their natural state. It also provides some of the most critical habitat for wolverines in the lower forty-eight states. In addition, healthy populations of bighorn sheep, mountain goats, elk, moose, mule deer, and whitetail deer are observable.

"Though this area is suitable for grizzly bears, no established populations are known to exist there."
—U.S. Forest Service

***

Soon after my son had been born, I had imagined this kind of opportunity—for an extended summer vacation with my boy. Years had now gone by since the notion first took hold, and my avenue of life had never quite led me to the circumstance and wherewithal to accomplish such a thing. New possibilities would open with promise, only to collapse with distraction. Missteps and more than a few failures had an endeavor such as this repeatedly just slip away. However, over the preceding four years or so, I'd finally gained some small traction. This year was shaping up to be the one. All the frustrations and blunders of the past could be compensated for. One grand adventure would solidify the dignity of my own fatherhood with my son.

Justin's mother and I had maintained a good relationship over the years since we'd decided that our marriage just didn't work for us, or our son. Though we still loved each other, we had not done well living with one another. Justin was a two-year-old when we began the Dad-every-other-weekend, alternating holidays, and three weeks of summer routine, as was worked out in our settlement. Deb remarried very soon to a stable and generous guy named Ken R. who suited her better, and they both supported keeping everyone on good terms. That had been fortuitous for me when my working career, financials, and emotional situations had struggled. Consequently, Justin and I had only used the summer vacation clause in abbreviated form a couple of times in the previous thirteen summers. This Father-Son Road Trip was to be a kind of restitution on my part, as I saw it; thus, it needed to be something dramatic. A western wilderness exploration looked to fit the bill.

The map indicated a route to our destination that would pass by multiple national and state parks, national monuments, historic sites, and cultural points of interest. My calculation was that the two thousand miles each way could be covered in four days, allowing plenty of time to check out whatever Justin or I decided was worth a look. Yellowstone National Park was an obvious attraction, where media had reported the reintroduction of the gray wolf to the wilds there, and record-breaking tourism traffic. It would not be a hard drive, since nearly the entire route followed interstate highways. My son was now old enough to help with some of the driving. There also were several spots that offered overnight practice-camping opportunities for us to sort ourselves out before entering the wilderness.

Inspired planning and provisioning proceeded steadily over the following three months. Checklists were compiled: preliminary tasks, items for purchase or borrowing, and what needed to be researched. Tent, sleeping bags, ax, canteen, clothing, on and on— even securing topographical maps with the trails to be hiked. I had contacted the tourism centers of the states we would pass through, who sent brochures of the attractions to see along the way.

Advice was sought from and freely given by friends and family. Some had done wilderness adventuring, but mostly it was folks who had just heard about the subject and shared their opinions about our plan. One of my oldest friends, Randall, was of strong opinion that I needed a firearm: "What, with bears, cougars, snakes, and wild mountain men about."

I did not own a firearm and had never had much inclination to have one. Randall persisted, attempting to set me straight by stating, "You just don't know who or what you will run up against out there, and do you think you should risk your son while being unarmed?"

Over the years, camping has become one of my most enjoyed recreational activities. Camping is fun! But there were also challenges from the beginning.

My first-time camping was in our backyard as a seven-year-old with my two younger brothers, John and Patrick. Dad had saved an old surplus canvas tent from his WWII campaign gear. He had served in the Pacific Theater and shared with us kids many a story at bedtime of his army experiences. Mom also served during WWII, but as an army nurse at a hospital within the States. For young boys, that was "girl-sounding stuff" and wasn't nearly as interesting. Mom conceded that Dad's stories might be more exciting to us, then, but promised we would appreciate her war stories more in a few years. She also reminded all, including my father, that she had been a lieutenant—an officer—while Dad had been drafted and was just a sergeant.

One mid-summer evening, after weeks of our whining to go camping, Mother finally pulled rank and told our dad to set up his WWII pup tent in our backyard. My brothers and I were thrilled. We could barely keep ourselves out from underfoot as he fashioned ground stakes and center poles. He then raised the shelter before our eyes. We outfitted our newly imagined frontier tent with blankets, flashlights, pillows, and Dad's authentic U.S. Army canteen full of Kool-Aid. Other essentials were our trusty toy six-gun pistols, cowboy hats, and lots of snacks, of course.

All went great that first hour. We watched the stars appear in the night sky while blinking lights of airplanes high overhead slowly passing by. The chirping of birds, buzzing of insects, and various routine sounds of the city became more distinctly audible as the light of day faded. We snuggled in our blankets, but that didn't mean sleep. The snacks were munched and the Kool-Aid guzzled. Then came multiple trips back into the house bathroom to relieve full little bladders, since peeing in the yard was forbidden. Flashlights snapped on and off as each new night sound surrounding the tent was identified or speculated about. All threats were vigorously fought off with rapid-fire six-gun action and our voicing of appropriate sound effects. Wild Indians, mountain lions, wolves, bears, outlaw desperadoes, and enemy soldiers were all slaughtered in a hail of six-shooter lead. Only obligatory, imaginary, TV-inspired "minor flesh wounds" were suffered by our side in these battles.

As the household lights of the neighborhood blinked off and the night turned darker still, all quieted down as we began to drowse. Immediate sleep didn't occur, though, like in the movies we'd seen. The ground was getting harder by the minute. After much fidgeting, complaints of each other's invasion of personal space, and frequent rolling back and forth, sleep did overcome the discomforts at last. But too soon and unexpectedly, our slumbers were painfully interrupted by my mother shaking us awake. Urgently she announced, "You have to get up and come into the house now. It's raining! You will get soaking wet. Come on, or you'll catch cold and be sick!"

We protested, as kids would, when our visions of being tough and rugged heroes in an adventure were thwarted. But we soon decided it may be for the best once the water seeped in. We were glad, for sure, as we ran back into the house to escape a cold, pelting Indiana rain, shivering to the bone. The tent had no flooring since, technically, it was just comprised of two half-shelter ponchos bound together. The inside flooded in the summer storm, drenching our clothes and blankets. We were clearly not prepared for rain.

There would be future episodes of outdoor camping to come. I would do the Boy Scout program, as would my five brothers, when their time came. Both of my parents were fully supportive of that participation, even though Dad had not been a Scout in his youth. An avenue of training in outdoor self-reliance and confidence-building would soon be revealed and explored. Other calamities would arise, where distinctions of precaution, preparedness, proper equipment, and execution of task would be taught and absorbed. Scouting was one of the most productive activities of my adolescent years, yet I'd had little opportunity to share any of this kind of experience with my son. That was now going to change.

Merriam-Webster defines namesake as one that has the same name as another; especially: one who is named after another or for whom another is named.

I became conscious of my father's importance sometime before two years of age by seeing photographs of him that my mother and aunt had displayed in our house. He was a person of possibility and mystery. I recall very much wanting to see him, but I was not allowed near due to the rules of the VA hospital where he was battling tuberculosis.

Dad had contracted TB while overseas in World War II. His first debilitating episode was three years before I was born, but he recovered after a year of hospital. He then suffered a serious relapse six weeks after I was born. Mom and her sister, my Aunt

Elvie, were my primary caregivers while he was away for two years. I recall once accompanying my mother and aunt in the car for a visit with Dad, but I wasn't allowed into the building and was very disappointed. Forced to stay outside, I stalked and chased a stray cat that was on the grounds for a little while, but the chilly evening and darkness soon ended the game. Memory of the incident includes a long, cold wait in the parked car with my aunt until Mother returned from visiting with Dad.

There is vague recollection of when my father did come home. I was just past two years of age and very excited with the anticipation of this grand event. My memory of the actual arrival was a big commotion of a large giant in pajamas and overcoat entering the front door and being helped through the living room to a bedroom by my mother. Aunt Elvie held me out of the way of his discernible struggle to pass through. He was still not fully recovered from the illness, and I recall watching him take bed rest for many days after arriving.

At first, he couldn't rise all day long, and I had very restricted interaction with him at his bedside. Later, once he had recovered enough to be up and about, his every activity became of astounding interest and an obsession to imitate. He was the new commanding presence of my environment, receiving much of the attentions that my mother had until then lavished on me. It was his voice and presence that was now dominant. But he seemed to like me most of the time.

Dad, Joseph McGuire, was my first hero in the world and would be the primary authority to be reckoned with for approval of all actions while growing up—and in later years, too. It would be on the shoulders of his standards, ideals, and accomplishments that I would formulate my own. It is clear to me now that what differences existed between us in those realms were of mostly articulation and emphasis, and very little difference in content. By broader definition, I am his namesake, with his surname and not the name of some other. With the name comes an identity, a grounding, and perhaps the first basis for personal aspirations, desires, and dreams. On this template, many of my goals in life would be created and acted upon.

Other heroes and role models would capture my imagination over the years from books, movies, television, and personal interactions. Presidents, explorers, astronauts, and musicians all captured my youthful fancy. But the first and most powerful was my dad. It was he who first ignited my hunger for adventure to rival his own, to risk and gamble against the odds, and demonstrated how important love of family is.

Organized sports, church groups, and summer camps provided some participatory venues for my youthful desires to learn and play the game or feel closer to the natural world. But on my first sight of a boy at school in a Scout uniform, it was clear that this kind of group was a cut above in realism and would be a very cool thing to do. The more I found out about it, the greater was my desire to participate. The prospect of living into adventures previously only real within my imagination finally had a path.

The Boy Scouts of America is a youth organization in the United States that began with the goal to train young people in responsible citizenship, character development, and self-reliance. Through participation in a wide range of outdoor activities and educational programs the Scout Method is taught. It is an informal education system, a "learning by doing," that works naturally and unconsciously. The boys are mentored and trained by more experienced Scouts of the group in the various skills of Scoutcraft, with the ultimate result that proficiency, teamwork, and real leadership occur.

Most of all, for me, it centered on the outdoor camping, where a city kid could be self-reliant out in the wilds. Scouting ultimately proved to be all I was promised and expected, as well as huge fun. Due to the many outdoor practical skills mastered and overall successes achieved in the program, my every confidence was that my son would become as enthused as I about this kind of recreation.

There was also an urgency to do this kind of event with my son this year. The car keys would soon be in his possession, and every parent can relate to that moment as a turning point in the relationship with their beloved child. His own blossoming agenda would grow with this new mobility and likely soon discount participation with mine. The vacation project seemed cast as a "now or never" proposition. This father-son activity would finally bring to bear some of the expertise I had acquired and wished to share from my own "Road to Eagle Scout." What better venue than a four-thousand-mile road trip into one of the largest wilderness areas in the lower forty-eight states? What could possibly go seriously wrong in the late twentieth century, if one is trained and prepared? I had Basketry Merit Badge, after all.

Robert Stephenson Smyth Baden-Powell is the man credited as the Founder of the Scouting Movement. He was a much-decorated general in the British Army who became famous during the Boer War in South Africa at the turn of the 20th century. He was also known as 1st Baron Baden-Powell, Lord Baden-Powell, and B-P for short.

Baden-Powell held the first camp outing for twenty boys at Brownsea Island of Great Britain in 1907. The event was a huge success, and coupled the following year with the publication of his manual, *Scouting for Boys*, youth organizations throughout the country and Ireland spontaneously formed Boy Scout troops.

Scouting soon came to the United States due to the efforts of an American publisher named William D. Boyce, who had met one of B-P's Scouts. The legend is that Mr. Boyce found himself lost in downtown London on a dark, foggy night. On meeting a young lad as he wandered the street, the boy offered to help the publisher find his way to his destination. When offered money for the assistance, the boy refused, declaring that his Scout Slogan is "*do a good turn daily*". Mr. Boyce was more than impressed. Scouts pledge to live by a Code of Honor.

Scouting is rooted in the historic old frontier traditions of training American youth. Many of the outdoor skills taught to this day were originally recorded by Baden-Powell from the very "real deal" American Wild West and international frontiersman, Frederick Russell Burnham. His was a life so dramatic, historically action-packed, and full of heroic accomplishments on two continents, that Hollywood and television have proved too small to profile his incredible life story. Burnham displayed the very kinds of personal exploits, aspects of character, and generosity of spirit that we attribute to our heroes of the past and hold forth to our youth and society at large to be emulated. It is he who is considered the Father of Scouting.

"Be Prepared" is the famous motto of the Boy Scouts, and many of life's failures can be attributed to ignoring or falling short of this maxim.

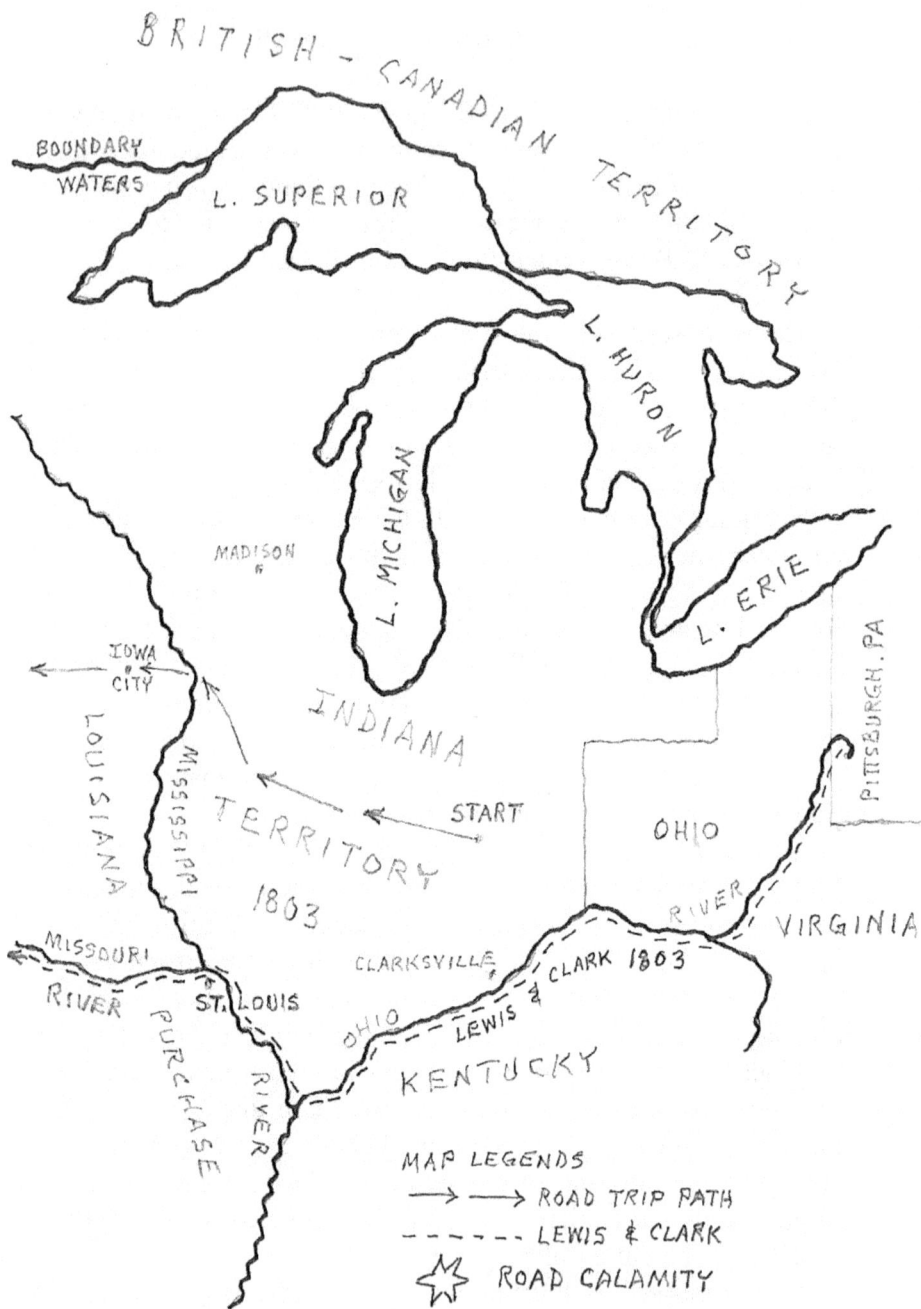

BRITISH - CANADIAN TERRITORY

BOUNDARY WATERS

L. SUPERIOR

L. HURON

L. MICHIGAN

MADISON

L. ERIE

PITTSBURGH, PA

IOWA CITY

LOUISIANA

MISSISSIPPI

INDIANA

TERRITORY

1803

START

OHIO

VIRGINIA

MISSOURI

RIVER

ST. LOUIS

PURCHASE

RIVER

CLARKSVILLE

OHIO

RIVER

LEWIS & CLARK 1803

KENTUCKY

MAP LEGENDS
→ ─ → ROAD TRIP PATH
─ ─ ─ ─ LEWIS & CLARK
☆ ROAD CALAMITY

CHAPTER
TWO

Road Trip 1, Day 1...

Behaviorists have said that it is rare that humans think thoughts more than five percent different from one day to the next. Human beings think nearly all repeated thoughts from the day before, and this can act as a mental conspiracy. The routines of working for money, being engaged in relationships, indulging in entertainments, and pacing ourselves to get through the day all require repetitions of thought, for the most part. When our routines are working well, we label that as "good," and the intended outcomes derived as being successful. More often than not, humans experience a sense of satisfaction from their successful intended outcomes. We describe routines that derive consistently successful outcomes as "being in the groove," to put an even better face on it, and we often feel like life itself is going well and nearly effortlessly. I call this a conspiracy of the "human life activity groove." Vacations demand different routines; thus, the established groove of routine life activity sometimes doesn't work so well.

The fact that our route would intersect the expeditionary trail of Lewis and Clark at several points was a most interesting bonus. Imagining the historical time of the Corps of Discovery overlaying our own, greatly sharpened the visual experiences. This road trip with my son had already been delayed a year due to last-minute logistics and priority of event scheduling issues. One might think that an extra full year would have allowed plenty of preparation to smooth out the unforeseen last-minute tasks required. Guess what? Maybe not so much. Delayed departure seems to always be embedded in any grand exploration, no matter the plan. A good case in point is the Louis and Clark Expedition of 1803 – 1806:

Captain Meriwether Lewis's optimistic intention was to depart up the Missouri River by August of 1803 and complete the exploration of the Louisiana Purchase the following year.

But delays bedeviled his intentions. His problems began with the primary mode of transport for moving up the river, a keelboat. It fell drastically behind construction schedule at its building site in Pittsburgh. This keelboat was a vessel of Lewis's own design, and more resembled a large galley with a sail than the traditional keelboats plying the rivers of that time. The shipbuilder was accused of constant drunkenness and sickness, the building crew went on strike, and the Ohio River was reported to be sinking to the lowest levels in memory due to severe drought. "Lewis says he 'went nearly mad with the delays, but held on because the job absolutely had to be done right.'"[4] His contractor was the only game in town, the only skilled shipwright west of the Appalachians, as inquiries about contracting someone else repeatedly confirmed.

When the craft was finally completed on the morning of August 31st, six weeks late, Lewis loaded the boat and was heading downriver within three hours. But sandbars in the low water restricted headway as the craft had to be dragged over them, and progress was very slow (just ten miles on the Ohio River that first day). The journey downstream took another six weeks to reach Clarksville, Indiana, where he picked up his co-captain, William Clark, and enlisted the first dozen recruits for the Expedition. They finally reached the town of Cahokia, Illinois, on the Mississippi River December 9th. St. Louis was on the opposite side of the river as was the mouth of the mighty Missouri River, the official starting point of discovery for the expedition. The men then built a winter camp close by to await the spring thaw, with a resumption date set for mid-April of 1804.

"On May 13th, 1804, William Clark reported that all was ready. The next morning, Clark's journal states, 'Fixing for a start.' He also related concerns that though they were provisioned with everything authorized, he felt that more was desirable."[5] Such were the constraints of time and a budget in those times as well as today. They took off later that afternoon, moving four miles upriver, and set up the first camp. The loaded boats then had to be repacked several times.

***

4 Ambrose

5 Ambrose

24

Justin and I had set a departure time (twelve o'clock noon on day one), but issues with fitting everything into the car, retracing transits from one house to another to retrieve what had been overlooked, repacking, and the underestimation of city traffic, all conspired to delay actual separation from town. My thoughts were that evil deities had conspired against us. Circumstances acted as a kind of invisible glue or muck in my groove. A mind-fog was also being emitted, intent on preventing escape from the clutches of the city and our human routines of life serving it.

This day was one of many and strenuous efforts, as my groove of practiced thought and daily activity struggled to transform to our new endeavor. The intended departure by noon slipped to one o'clock, three o'clock, and later still. Every street signal switched to red on approach, and every turn from one street to the next confronted endless fence-lines of oncoming car traffic, prohibiting advance.

Still, we were pumped with adrenalin and boldly on the highway by 3:45 P.M. and feeling elated about it. Delayed lunch of delicious sandwiches, chips, fruit, cookies, and soft drinks were finally consumed while driving "Westward Ho!" Energetic proteins and sugars buzzed within us as the miles began to click by, heading west at last.

The sun was beginning to set after passing through Peoria, Illinois, so it was past time for dinner and a break as we rolled into Davenport, Iowa in the twilight before dark. Our first major geological feature of the North American continent, the Mississippi River, was ensconced in darkness and only vaguely discernible by the illumination of the bridge and other isolated and dispersed lights on the far shore. Admiration of this waterway of continental importance in American and Native American history, and to world geography, would have to await the return leg of our adventure.

Truck stop diners are often the best food available when on the road, but our first experience fell well short of our hopes. "Sucked," in fact, says my journal. Back on the highway, we drove on another hour, but by eleven o'clock we were both spent. A motel at one of the Iowa City exits was the choice for this night's rest. I'd been running full throttle for eighteen hours on three hours of sleep from the previous night, and I'd had only four temper upsets about traffic for the day. That was a good day. Slept like a rock.

Day 2...

Big plans for this day had us out of bed by six o'clock in the morning and back on the road after a large breakfast, gas fill-up, and a minor adjustment to the engine shroud, which had loosened and was scraping beneath the vehicle a bit. The miles again clicked by as we easily crossed the state of Iowa to the Council Bluffs bypass on the eastern bank of the Missouri River, just across from Omaha, Nebraska. There, was located a rest stop that served perfectly as a good place to eat lunch.

Out from our well-stocked travel cooler we pulled lunch meats, potato salad, coleslaw, condiments, and soft drinks to quench our famished appetites. The location was secluded and fairly quiet, with only occasional road traffic passing by out of sight. The conversation was muted as we munched our food. As we did a second stretching of our legs to the facility I announced we should begin Justin's driving lessons at the next opportunity.

Continuing north, the roadway ran parallel to the river. The water could not be observed however, due to the highway having been built three to four miles away and above the floodplain to prevent roadway flooding. An hour later, the signs of Sioux City came into view through some light rain. Sgt. Charles Floyd would be the only fatality suffered by the Lewis and Clark Corps of Discovery, and he was buried there by the river. Prominent signs to a monument of commemoration were well posted. The rain dampened our enthusiasm for that to be our first attraction stop, however.

It was there, however, in an empty area of a parking lot that I sought to teach my son the art of driving a manual transmission. Justin had taken courses and earned a student driver's license. His mother assured me he was quite adept at the new privilege while driving her automatic. He was eager for the training and I was willing, even though the car engine had been running a bit roughly. The recent tune-up and double inspection had eased any fears, and his driving assistance would lighten my load considerably. Switching seats and strapping in, he started the car before I could warn to shift out of gear.

Ride 'em cowboy! ... and we began as the car bucked forward and then stalled. My late instruction to start the car while out of gear brought a quick laugh as he complied with his second attempt.

"Now, keep depressing the clutch pedal and add a little gas." Varoom went the engine.

I continued guidance. "Good! Back off the gas a little, put the shifter in first gear, and slowly ease up on the clutch." Grinding gears ate themselves. "Push in the clutch pedal more." The grinding stopped and the engine RPMs sank.

"Little more gas…" and RPMs surged… "and put the shifter in gear…" more grinding, but then we had full engagement as he depressed the clutch pedal with more extension.

"Slowly ease up on the clutch and give a little more gas." RPMs rose and the car bucked forward, but the engine didn't stall, and we were accelerating.

"Slow down, ease up a little…keep left away from the parking lot light pole."

Justin turned, but also braked too hard, and the car bucked to a stop as the engine died out.

"That was good, Son. Next time remember to depress the clutch at the same time as you brake. You did great for a first time. Let's try again."

While repeating the process several more times, but with new variations producing near-duplicate outcomes of stalling the car, the rain continued to patter down. With each restart, the engine seemed to roughen a bit more and took more than one ignition attempt to re-fire. Concerns of depleting the battery after about twenty minutes had me gently suggest that perhaps we could call the first lesson complete. We did need to get going down the road again and could do another lesson tomorrow. After all, this practice was not really under ideal conditions. The car was over packed with our travel and camping gear, and the rain added real distraction. Justin agreed, clearly disappointed, but also appearing relieved to end this obviously frustrating first attempt. We switched seating and continued onward into South Dakota, toward Sioux Falls and the wider open spaces beyond.

Given how numerous and pervasive automobiles are in the United States, I was mildly surprised to learn that it was a German named Karl Benz who holds the consensus title of: "Inventor of the modern automobile, or horseless carriage." Given the huge network of highways clogged with American vacationers every summer, engaged in their own road trips of pleasure and business, the bigger surprise was that it was Benz's wife, Bertha, who conducted the first recorded long-distance road trip. Without her husband's consent or knowledge—or power steering—she "borrowed" Karl's third manufactured vehicle.

Bertha loaded her two teenage sons, Richard and Eugene, into the car and traveled from Mannheim to Pforzheim, Germany, and back, for a distance of sixty-six miles. The car's maximum speed was just ten miles per hour. She said she went to visit her mother. The bio doesn't mention whether the boys received their driving lessons on the journey, but history rates the trip a huge success for advertising Karl's invention. Once the word got out, the vehicle sales increased greatly and his enterprise evolved into the Mercedes-Benz automobile company. Yet more evidence that behind a successful man is a strong woman.[6]

***

I stared in dazed disbelief at the dashboard as my hands still gripped the steering wheel, an acrid odor of burnt oil permeating the cabin of our now silent vehicle. Moments before, Justin and I had been congratulating ourselves on the smooth sailing and excellent travel time we were making up, driving comfortably at seventy miles per hour on I-90, westward into the sun. The disjointed and late departure of our vacation looked to be smoothing out, finally conforming to plan. Any satisfaction proved fleeting, however, when a sudden, audible, metallic "clank" issued from the front of the car. Power disappeared immediately, and the vehicle coasted to a full stop alongside the near-empty highway. Repeated turns of the key generated no sound from even the radio, and small whiffs of black smoke oozed from the front hood.

Though sometimes described as volatile by others, I still would characterize my responses that followed as measured, restrained, or appropriate to the circumstance. My thorough fist-pounding of the steering wheel lasted less than a minute and did not break it. Shouting the seven-words-you-can't-say-on-TV-without-getting-bleeped (liberally punctuated with several "*dammits!*") at the top of my lungs only lasted until the second polite request by my son, calmly sitting as the quiet passenger, to "please stop the rant." My mental paralysis dwelling on the fact that we were marooned in

6 Bertha-Benz Memorial Route Official Website

the wide open of the Northern Great Plains lasted only another two or three minutes—tops. Besides, everyone (including my son) had heard those seven words before. The passionate, high-volume attributions to inanimate object, animals, and famous personages, as well as my inventive variations of sequence, were a lesson in "venting."

After re-opening my eyes and calmly wiping bits of spittle from the steering wheel, windshield, and dashboard areas, my clearing vision focused on the trip odometer, which read 865 miles, and then the clock indicating 6:05 P.M. Central Savings Time. I then exited the car and looked under the hood at the silent power plant. An oily cloud of steam obscured the view and I could discern little. I did assess a strong probability that the engine was blown with a thrown rod and the car was done. It was a twelve-year-old Honda Accord with 139,000 miles. It was an automobile well renowned for reliability and longevity. My vehicle had so far lived up to that reputation. Steady maintenance was my rule over the years. Two extensive inspections and a tune-up had been part of meticulous vacation preparations. But my hometown mechanic's final assurance, "That engine is very strong," was now a bitter recollection from our conversation five days earlier.

We needed a telephone, and a highway exit was about half-a-mile ahead. Visible were building structures on both sides of the bridge overpass that might be occupied farmhouses. We agreed it better that Justin stay with the car, in case a highway patrol or passerby stopped to assist while I was away. So, off I went walking into what felt like "the middle of nowhere." With each step, my mind ticked off the evidence, circumstance, and options.

Oil is splattered all over the engine and under the hood, so the thing is probably blown. Look for help, but what kind? ... a tow? …a repair? …bus tickets? What will we do with all our stuff in the car? …Damn, this hike is farther than it looks.

It was some ten minutes to reach the closest house, and after several knocks on the door, I determined it was empty or nobody was home. Crossing over the highway bridge, the car was not too distant to see Justin's silhouette within, but he didn't respond to my wave. His thoughts I could not imagine. Continuing to the second farmhouse, again there was no response from inside. The last house across the road appeared even less likely to be inhabited, but then I heard an engine start up over there. I could see a woman riding a lawn mower about the property. So, over there I walked, with quiet fears and desperation, alongside hope that help would be granted.

She was startled by my sudden appearance, not noticing as I had walked close enough for my third hello to be heard over the mower noise. It was as if my worst fears were momentarily realized as her head turned to me with eyes blazing. Putting on the best smile I could compose (trying for friendly innocence to cover extreme embarrassment, like being confronted for accidentally entering the wrong public rest room), I introduced myself and my problem. A sympathetic smile gradually replaced her guarded expression as she heard my tale of woe. In response to my request to borrow their telephone, she replied that perhaps her husband might help me. Dismounting her mower, she walked me over toward a barn on the property. Her husband, having seen me, the intruder, was already walking over to meet us. He listened to my situation with authentic concern, and then unhesitatingly invited me into their home. His wife accompanied us and offered a glass of water while he immediately started making calls for the needed towing service from the adjoining room.

Karl and Gretchen were quite a handsome young couple in their early thirties who had purchased their farm just two years prior, as I learned from our small talk. He was a clean, taller-than-average man with pale blond hair, while she was of medium height, darker hair, and an athletic build. They had two young children, a boy and a girl, who appeared pre-school aged. The interior of their home was neat and tidy, well furnished, with the smell of dinner wafting from the kitchen. A Little House on the Prairie, updated to the doorstep of the twenty-first century. They were also well within the character of being most kind and generous.

After twenty minutes of my sharing conversation with his wife, Karl rejoined us and reported that it had taken him three calls to locate a towing service, but one was finally en route. He declined my offer to pay any long-distance charges he may have incurred and invited me to stay with them to await the tow truck. With much thanks, I expressed my concern to get back to my son at the car, who'd been there alone all the while. Karl immediately offered to drive me back to the vehicle, which I readily accepted. After thanking Gretchen for her hospitality, Karl and I departed the house and climbed into his pickup truck. He promptly returned me to the stranded Honda as the clock ticked 7:12 P.M. Justin and I then watched our only confirmed link to rescue drive away.

Darkening thoughts matched a now overcast sky. My conversation with Justin was no brighter as I reviewed the situation again, ticking off the limited choices available to us if the car had embraced its mortality. Justin was more the optimist, expressing confidence in a good outcome, and in his dad. A Scout is cheerful. He declared that he was sure all would work out okay. I dared not think that possible, afraid to jinx us even worse at this point.

The car had come to a stop next to a small pond within a cornfield next to the roadside. Several wild birds, including ducks, were congregating there as the end of day drew on. We watched them for a while, commenting on both those birds recognized and not. Cows were

Storm clouds

way out in a pasture area we could see, but the other fields were cultivated with more corn or soy beans. Counting passing vehicles was very slow business, with five- and ten-minute intervals often between them. We watched a strange yellow beacon light far ahead, blinking through a shroud of thickening mist, as the clock ticked, ticked, and we waited and waited.

"Where is that guy with the tow?" we wondered and finally spoke aloud.

The clock now read 8:10 P.M., the overcast skies had turned to rain clouds sprinkling drops at a growing pace, and the western winds were picking up velocity. I had just declined a last-minute offer for a ride to find help, from the only vehicle that stopped for us. Second thoughts regarding the wisdom of that choice were now racing between my ears as I watched the storm close in. The blinking yellow beacon ahead was no longer visible. The warning was over.

Black serpent tongues licked down from at least three low-hanging, black funnel-shaped clouds. The weather front was quickly approaching us head-on from the horizon ahead. Like primordial beasts of perdition, the funnel clouds marched across the rural tableland while rain fell more intensely, splattering the windshield and roof with large, loud drops, whose individual impacts soon merged into a roar. Visibility disappeared into a pulsing, solid sheet of water on the glass. Justin and I watched the half-matured corn in the surrounding fields bow repeatedly horizontal in spastic jerks from the wind gusts.

Our only shelter from this howling outburst of nature was now a small, cramped, very broken and dead-on-the-road compact sedan, crammed to the max with all the accouterment, supply, and dreams of our grand expedition. Audible conversation was overwhelmed. My thoughts alternated between brief, progressive visions of weathering the storm to those of fatal disaster. The worst: a tornado touching down on the car, getting pulled airborne, the doors and glass crushed, exploded, the contents within, including Justin and I, ejected out, maimed and scattered on the surrounding fields. The bigger probability: a rescue of sorts, eventually, a premature end to Dave's Incredible Adventure, and returning home on a Greyhound bus. Vehicle abandoned junk, tail between my legs, shamed irrevocably in the eyes of my family, friends, and worst of all, my son.

"Justin, fasten your seatbelt!" I said, voice raised over the din outside. I explained that being belted inside the car during a tornado had better survival odds, by at least a few points, than the other option. I concluded: "Not much, probably, but ya do what ya can do." We both buckled up. It was like being trapped in the tornado scene in The Wizard of OZ, a child's nightmare, and I was that stupid Dorothy character…this foolish vacation idea, this adolescent over-reach, a self-inflicted calamity of my own making…*She-i-i-i-i-t!* This was failure…again…and it was going from bad to worse with each tick of the clock.

The storm front began passing directly overhead. We were then in the middle of it! A blinding lightning bolt struck the field very close, one hundred feet to our right with an instantaneous ear-splitting crack, followed by a deep booming echo of thunder vibrating our nerve endings. The blowing wind and rain buffeted and rocked the car. Within another minute, a second lightning bolt flashed, cracked, and boomed. A kind of resignation and surrendering to fate flooded my mind as I watched the rain pounding the glass.

Then, abruptly, the furious winds and rain faded into a whimper and a drizzle. The windshield cleared to reveal a brightened sky. The precipitation stopped within a few more minutes, and small birds could be seen flying out from their own shelters. The mysterious blinking yellow light reappeared just above the horizon. Justin remarked that a rainbow was visible behind us. Turning to observe the rainbow, I watched the dark skies of the storm galloping east and away. Did the spirit of Dorothy click the heels of her magic shoes? "There's no place like home" most definitely had passed through our minds.

Karl, good on his word, soon rolled up alongside us in his pick-up truck. "You guys are still here? Didn't the tow truck show up?" His shocked exasperation rivaled our own.

My negative response to his second question produced a few words I couldn't quite hear as he slightly shook his head back and forth. He then called out that he would go back home and telephone again. A Scout is kind. We were just sitting back after watching him cross the overpass bridge and out of sight when I noticed flashing lights in the rearview mirror. The tow truck was pulling up behind us, finally. It was 8:55 P.M.

Larry of Larry's Tow Service had arrived at last. We all gathered at the Honda's hood as Larry inspected the engine, listening to my rendition of the breakdown story. He disagreed with my belief that the engine was blown and said he thought it was the timing belt inside the engine that may have given out. Larry continued that he couldn't recommend his own shop for the repair because they didn't work on imported cars. I would need a Honda dealership to do this kind of repair. The nearest dealer would be some fifty miles back in Sioux Falls. "What would you like to do?"

Easy answer: about-face and forward march to the rear, back to civilization…an all-night cafe for food…a hotel bed…and a Honda dealer car fix, provided the money held out...or, if necessary, a bus station.

***

The relationship my father had experienced with my grandfather while growing up had never been one talked about much, and what little that was said left me, as the listener, with a sadness. Dad says Grandfather's relationship with him in his early years was not close but had eventually drawn closer in his later teen years. My father didn't tell any stories of he and his dad having fun together. Dad said he had decided to be more closely involved with his own kids in their earlier years than his own father had been with him. Grandfather was described as a nice guy, and that was pretty much where the subject would end.

Grandfather had created and grown a road building company during and after the First World War, and achieved a great deal of prosperity prior to the Great Depression. Fortune frowned on him with that great national disaster. He, like millions of other Americans, was wiped out, bankrupted, and lost his home ownership, car, and all the nicer things of an upper middle-class living he had worked very long and hard for. Repeated failures to revive the business devastated him, reducing him to picking up small odd jobs for meager income, and he turned more and more to alcohol as a last resort to escape the ruin he saw his life had become.

My father was not quite ten years old when the stock market crashed, and he was to become an early contributor to the household income. He delivered newspapers, cut neighbors' grass, shoveled snow, and even collected recyclable glass soda and beer bottles to earn what money he could. In his teen years, my father would help with some of the paying odd jobs my grandfather did manage to find, often of the handyman variety. That is where Dad declares his real relationship with his father began.

Being drafted in 1941 changed his Great Depression hardscrabble life. Dad was among the first shipped out to the South Pacific to be part of General McArthur's "Return to the Philippine Islands Campaign." At war's end, the G.I. Bill solved the college money problem. He attended Notre Dame University and earned a degree in architecture, but battling tuberculosis in his third year of school delayed completion of his studies for an extra year.

Dad had met my mom during his college years after the war, and she would visit him while he was recovering at the VA hospital. He still made a good enough impression that she married him shortly after he was discharged from the hospital, healthy and fit once again. I showed up ten months later. Mom and Dad celebrated their first marriage anniversary back at the VA hospital due to my father's TB relapse.

Relationship is the central passport to living a life as a human being. We create relationships, grow them, and choose to maintain those we value in order to keep them viable. This maintenance also implies the often-uncomfortable requirement of repairing them. My dad and I were in the repair business for the most part.

One of those successful repair chapters was his unrestrained but also cautious support of me in Scouting, and we both got what we wanted: for me to thrive. The greater part of the rest of our father-son chapters seemed to be of mistakes, miscommunication, and errors. Our familiarity would breed distrust, upset, rebellion, and even an occasional experience of contempt.

With my own son, absence appeared to have allowed the heart to grow fonder. Debby would often complain over the years that Justin always viewed me as the "good guy," and it was unfair to them both. It certainly was for her. But that is also a double-edged sword. My experience was that of missing the vast majority of Justin's day-to-day growing up, most of his participations in sports, school, friends, and the un-programmed, sometimes special daily interactions of the family household I had started, and lost.

I saw myself as having fallen way short of providing at least what I had been provided. Never mind my long-held vow to myself, to be a different kind of father than my own had been with me. I'd accomplished that in spades! But career, money, marriage, and personal accomplishment had all fallen out of sight of my aspirations. I was just barely holding on to this second chance at parenthood by the skin of my teeth. The mirror was not showing a pretty reflection. My life, at this time, seemed near the point of the Steely Dan lyric: "They got a name for all the winners in the world, and I want a name when I lose…"

There was a lot of extra baggage riding in that car with me.

CALAMITY TRAIL

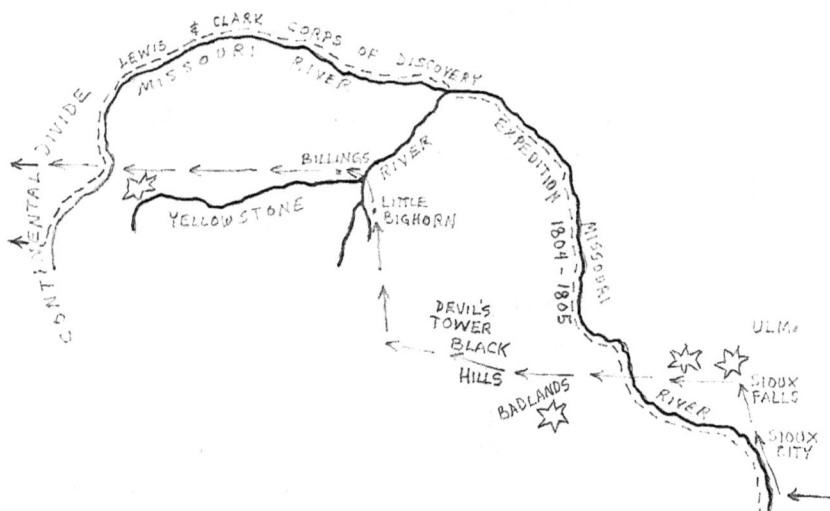

CHAPTER THREE

Day Three...

This day started at seven o'clock in the morning with the telephone ringing a wake-up call from the motel's front desk. The urgency to get up and going was underlined with residual stress born from the events of the preceding day. The car had indeed been towed to Sioux Falls, South Dakota. The keys had been stuffed in a night drop-off slot with a short note describing what had happened, my uneducated guess of the problem, and my promise to call for a 7:30 A.M. consult. A shower did wonders for clearing the mind and revitalized hope that the journey would continue.

Scott, the service manager of the dealership, was on the telephone by 7:45 A.M. and spoke with optimistic confidence, stating that his guys were already investigating the cause of the vehicle's failure. He would call back with a diagnosis of the problem and solution, if there was one, within the next forty-five minutes.

Lord Baden-Powell didn't have the perfect childhood, as one may imagine. His father died when Robert was three years old, and he says, "The whole secret of my getting on lay with my mother." She raised and inspired him well in his early years, for he was awarded a scholarship to attend the prestigious Charterhouse Public School. It was there that his Scouting skills began. Accounts of his life mention that to avoid his academic teachers, he would often sneak off-campus to stalk, trap, and cook wild game animals in the strictly out-of-bounds woods nearby. Robert was also active during holidays, adventuring outdoors on yachting and canoeing expeditions with his older brothers.

Baden-Powell joined the British Army after completing his schooling in 1876 as a cavalry officer. He was firstly stationed in India-Pakistan near Afghanistan, and later in South Africa, honing his military scouting skills amidst the Zulu. Promotions over time brought Robert his own commands during the British suppressions of other native uprisings in Rhodesia, the West African Gold Coast, and back in South Africa again. When the Second Boer War broke out in 1899, he was on the frontier of the Boer Republic. B-P found himself with his cavalry unit surrounded and seriously outnumbered by a Boer army at the town of Mafeking, South Africa. Rather than destroy a large quantity of supplies and retreat, he held out until his men were forced to eat their horses. The siege lasted 217 days until relief arrived, thus Robert became a national hero and soon was promoted to general.

During the siege, an auxiliary unit known as the Mafeking Cadet Corps assisted, and it comprised white boys not old enough to fight. They stood guard duty, carried messages, assisted in hospitals, and so on, freeing the grown men to fight. B-P must have been impressed with their performance. It is this Cadet Corps that was used as an "*object lesson of courage and the equanimity with which to perform tasks,*" as quoted in Baden-Powell's first Boy Scout manual. Upon returning from the war, Baden-Powell was still an active duty officer holding the rank of Lieutenant-General when he founded the Scout Movement, so the first edition of the *Scouting for Boys* manual published a year later still retained a few hard edges from a previous military scouting version.

B-P explains:

"The Scout Motto is: BE PREPARED, which means you are always in a state of readiness in mind and body to do your DUTY."

"Be Prepared in Mind by having disciplined yourself to be obedient to every order, and also by having thought out beforehand any accident or situation that might occur, so that you know the right thing to do at the right moment, and are willing to do it."

"Be Prepared in Body by making yourself strong and active and able to do the right thing at the right moment, and do it."

"To do the right thing at the right moment" can be extreme: "Where a man has gone so far as to attempt suicide, a Scout should know what to do with him." B-P also remarked in his Scout Manual that "Most people at one time or the other in their lives get a feeling that they will kill themselves…" and recommended that a Scout should be a friend to people in such crisis.

"BE PREPARED to die for your country if need be, so that when the moment arrives you may charge home with confidence, not caring whether you are going to be killed or not."

One of the early recommended skills for boys was "Life-Saving, but this was not only about saving someone from drowning. It could also be how to prevent a man shooting another with a pistol."

The telephone call from Scott confirmed the engine timing belt speculation, and he promised to have the car running like new for three hundred dollars. His offer to pick us up from the hotel at ten o'clock that morning was promptly accepted. Allowing my son to sleep a bit later, I went across the street to the diner and loaded up on three cups of coffee caffeine, a five-cigarette nicotine dose, and paged through a *USA Today*. By 10:15 A.M., I had collected Justin, completed room check-out, and was on the telephone in the motel lobby with the dealership inquiring, "Where is the ride?"

Scott reported more problems. "The timing belt was fixed, but not the motor head gasket or the lower timing belt, which should also be replaced. Those parts are out of stock and there was some difficulty re-assembling, but we will get it done somehow."

A driver arrived fifteen minutes later, and at the dealership my car was declared road worthy and ready to go…sort of.

Scott explained, "The engine still has a small oil leak and is starting a bit rough, but it should definitely be good for the eight hundred miles back home to Indianapolis," all with a prideful grin on his face.

I questioned, "Is the car good for a strong eight hundred miles?"

He answered, "Oh, yeah, the car will be very strong and can go quite a bit farther than that."

"Does that mean the car might be good for a couple of thousand miles?"

The service manager kept smiling but his eyes did a quick roll. He would only concede that, "It might." Scott was not going that far with a guarantee, and, in fact, "Two thousand might be a push."

After a long pause, as the implications of the report settled, I concluded the interview, "Okay, fine…thanks…now where do I pay?"

As Justin and I were once again twentieth-century highway mobile and making our way to the Interstate, we discussed our situation quickly. The fork in the road was dead ahead. It really came down to answering one question with two options. "Do we play it safe and head back home, or push on despite the risk of playing out this scenario again in perhaps worse circumstances?"

Justin answered for both of us. "Let's go for it!"

Frederick Russell Burnham was born about 150 miles east of Sioux Falls, outside the frontier farming town of New Ulm, Minnesota. His father, Edwin, was a Presbyterian missionary to the Dakota Sioux Indian reservation nearby. The American Civil War had just broken out the month before his birth, and in the following year, many of the militia and U.S. Army units protecting the frontier had been reassigned east and south to that conflict. For years, the Indians had been cheated and abused by the government agents and traders who were to perform the treaty obligations, and they had suffered continued white-man encroachments on their subsistence wild-game hunting preserves. By August of 1862, the failure of the U.S. Government to give promised money and food deliveries had driven many of the Sioux to starvation, desperation, and a murderous mind. An insurrection broke out, known as the Dakota War of 1862, and that provided early drama to young Frederick's life.

While his father was twenty miles away procuring ammunition in the town of Mankato, Indians with war bonnets and paint were spotted in the surrounding woods by his mother approaching their cabin. She realized that it would be impossible to escape and hide while carrying a baby, so she hid Frederick in the cornfield within a basket, covered him with green corn husks, and then fled for her life. The next day, she returned with armed neighbors to the smoking ruin of their cabin, but found Fred where she had left him, unharmed and sleeping, still covered by the husks. Their house had been burned down, along with most of the town of New Ulm and hundreds of other outlying homesteads in the area. Well over four hundred white settlers were killed by the Indian surprise attacks of the first few days, while scores of others were kidnapped hostages. His father became one of those prominent in the defense of the town and helped to prevent its total destruction.

Burnham's dad suffered serious injury after the Indian uprising while rebuilding the family home, and his health deteriorated in the harsh Minnesotan winters. In hopes of making his life a little easier, he moved the family to Los Angeles, California, in 1870. Tuberculosis had set in, however, and he died two years later, leaving the family destitute. An uncle in Iowa offered to take them in but sent no travel money. A friend in L.A. eventually loaned them funds to buy railroad tickets for the journey, but young eleven-year-old Frederick refused to go back. He insisted on staying, getting a job to help support his family, and pay back the loan. His mother and baby brother did make the return trip, while Frederick stayed in California, got a job to make his own way, and repaid the loan by the time he was fourteen.

***

On the road west, with the noon-time sun high overhead, we charged. The Honda gradually lost most of its cough and sputter. My ear listened with keen acuity to every nuance of the engine, while my foot pressed the gas pedal to sixty-five miles an hour and became an extra sensor for every vibration. The occasional shuddering signaled by the steering wheel, vibration of the gas pedal, and cough of the engine gradually fell mostly still and silent, and we proceeded past the fateful mile-marker that had stopped us the previous evening. Thoughts of deep-felt appreciation and thanks went out to the Good Samaritan farmer there. Unfortunately, moving summer road construction obstructed the exit to their farm and prevented my planned stop there to express my personal thanks once again. I promised myself to do that on our return, no matter the ultimate outcome.

Visually admiring new physical landscape and geography passing by one's vehicle, that is different from what one is accustomed to, usually has a calming and entertaining effect. This often gives the traveler a long-term memory of scenic wonder, pleasure, and satisfaction, despite whatever tensions or distractions are occurring. The surrounding topography of the highway we had traversed since beginning the journey, however, looked little different from what we were used to back home. It was further homogenized by the national chain commercial businesses with their familiar advertising signage. Indiana is mostly flatlander country. A friend of mine had once described driving the Interstate

Highway between her city and mine as the most boring two-hundred-mile road in the country, with only one hill and two turns. Our western route had shown up as a similar description for the first 850 miles.

The North American Great Plains extend well east of the Mississippi River, across the northern halves of Illinois, Indiana, and Ohio, and used to be mostly grasslands, just like in the west. I've often read that bountiful wild game of deer, antelope, and up to seven million bison, known as the Eastern Herd, grazed and roamed prior to settlement by European immigrants in the eighteenth and early nineteenth centuries. The area is part of the larger physiographic province of the United States known as the Central Lowlands, and it stretches westward almost to the Missouri River. Glaciers covered this flattened land, and the small hills and gentle rolls of the surface that are visible are due to occasional glacial deposit areas and erosion by the drainage of rivers and streams. All the miles covered thus far had fallen short of what the term "Scenic West" had conjured up for our expectations. Some unusual and eye-catching signage repeating along I-90 did begin to distract from the mundane, however, and even provoked an occasional tickle.

The first was a succession of politically inspired signs comprising phrases completing a sentence, defending the rights of wild game hunters to continue exercising their right to put meat on the table and harvest fur animals for the pelts. A "stick it in the eye" message to the folks in animal rights groups who were voicing proposals to ban fur coats was the clear and brazen message.

Another series of signage we began to chuckle at was for a self-described, famous attraction named Wall Drug, the signs appearing every twenty-mile interval or so, with a different off-beat reason to come patronize it.

Then, a third and unusually large billboard said, "Come See the World-Famous Corn Palace." This was something that sounded so hokey, we just had to check it out. Perhaps it was due to our own state being well within the Corn Belt.

Our first tourist side venture exceeded all expectations. It was a large two story building near the town center, with huge wall murals covering the entire exterior, made entirely from multiple colored ears of corn. The building was also a museum. More and stunningly intricate murals made of corn were inside, and also excellent historical exhibits—vivid portrayals of the determination and grit of pioneers who settled and tamed that part of the country. A photographic gallery adorned the facility of the yearly transformations of the wall murals themselves. It was a magnificent display like no other. Brand new murals are constructed every year, requiring thousands of hours of effort and commitment.

Near the parking area was a line of souvenir kiosks selling jewelry, clothing, postcards, and even metal pans for would-be gold miners. We were still over three hundred miles shy of the Black Hills goldfields, but the allure of quick wealth available, by just panning gravel from a mountain stream, couldn't be sold soon enough to those who might catch the fever.

I scored my best souvenir there: An embroidered T-shirt. What we thought to be just a quick drive-by consumed nearly two hours!

We hit back on the road again, and the land topography soon began to change with each mile. Uninterrupted tableland fields of cash crop corn, soy beans, and wheat were broken with more frequent tracts of pasture, while the hills grew larger and clearly identifiable butte formations appeared. The Great Plains began transforming to the more arid prairie that would stretch onward another nine hundred miles to within the foothills of the Rocky Mountains. The sizable stands of trees and wooded sections, constituting occasional islands of green on the plains, shrank down to small, isolated copses of scrub growth and single trees that became fewer and farther between. Soon, we arrived at the second major geographic marker of our journey, and "dramatic" is a fair description of the Missouri River Valley at this point on the continent. We pulled over for an extended viewing.

"This is more like it!" Justin's satisfied exclamation once again expressed for the both of us the sensations triggered within as we beheld the panorama of the nearly four-hundred-foot-deep river valley from its eastern side. Our view extended for at least seventy-five miles, and the sky, studded with white cloud and the afternoon sun seemed larger than any we had ever seen before. Picnic tables at an overlook by the rest area proved a most perfect lunch stop for which our travel cooler was well prepared.

Meriwether Lewis and William Clark had bivouacked their Corps of Discovery for two days within our view, just across the river at a tributary creek they named Corvus, and the present town site of Oacoma, South Dakota. The journal that Louis kept describes the lands of the Missouri as that of rich soil and minerals, lush vegetation, and a hunter's paradise for harvesting nature's bounty of fish and wild game. Dated in mid-September of 1804, the notation was written while on their way north up the river, the Expedition being nearly a year behind schedule. Within a week of their stopping at this place, they would encounter the fearsome Teton Sioux Indian Tribe. Of all Indians west of the Mississippi, they declared them the only potential enemies of the American Government.

The rest stop there has since expanded to include a marvelous museum dedicated to the Corps of Discovery's passage. Within are multiple historical displays depicting the explorers' equipment, accoutrements, photographs, and storied accounts of those times and settlement afterward. Also, and most grand, is an authentic scale reproduction of Lewis's special keel boat, or river galley. An amazing factoid is that this vessel was within inches in size of the Pinta, Christopher Columbus's ocean vessel that first crossed the Atlantic and later returned to Spain in 1492.

Kevin Costner's movie, *Dances with Wolves*, does a wonderful job of bringing to the big screen the awesome majesty that the plains and prairie lands west of the Missouri Valley can stir in one's being. Each mile westward matched ever more closely the scenic rolling background lands used in the movie. At one point, we could see the very background panorama filmed to depict a bison herd grazing prior to stampeding during an Indian buffalo hunt action scene. Some estimates of the bison herds west of the Mississippi count upwards of sixty million of these animals roaming this land before the white-man intrusion. Close by, there was a viewable reproduction of the western town film set used in the movie.

By the time we neared the Badlands National Park, it was late in the day, the car was still running balky and tenuous, and it had not yet proven itself dependable to start the next morning. We opted to push on to Rapid City at the edge of the Black Hills to stay in close proximity to the auto services located there. Additionally, we would be near a whole menu of attractions near this town that we well may've chosen to settle for if we had a changed heart. This was one last chance for prudence to overcome our reckless determination to see the trip through to Idaho. Regardless, speaking of menus, I was ready for a couple of drinks, and Justin wanted a steak dinner.

Day Four…

Rising early on in the morning, which is a big deal for a teenager on vacation, the departure from Rapid City proved later than planned for. First on a list of to-dos was to locate a vehicle service center. The small oil leak required regular replenishment. Walmart offered a quick solution to this necessity, as well as the purchase of my long-missing sunglasses. Then we began looking over a few brochures of the local sights and attractions in the area. Mount Rushmore, Historic Deadwood, and a large aeronautic museum at Ellsworth Air Force Base beckoned as worthy places to check out.

After some debate, we voted to continue onward. However, we decided to get away from the Interstate and take a slower, more forested mountain State highway to view some of the scenic valleys within the Black Hills. Our route meandered via a northern access to Devil's Tower, progressing about one hundred miles over into Wyoming. This gigantic and very strange geological edifice was the first-declared United States National Monument back in 1906 by President "Teddy" Roosevelt, who's known as the country's first national resource preservation activist.

How this unusual "natural" formation took shape is a different story according to whomever you talk to. Geologists speculate that this tower was formed by an igneous intrusion of earth's deep subterranean mantel into the surface sedimentary rock layers, and perhaps is an eroded remnant of a laccolith. The igneous material that forms the tower is a phonolite porphyry, which intruded about forty million years ago. Granite! Supposedly, as the heated magma cooled, the granite cracked and formed into the hexagonal (sometimes four-, five-, and seven-sided) columns. Over the years, the surrounding sedimentary rock layers sank and eroded away, leaving the tower. Wow, was that theoretical explanation thick?

Another theory is that the tower is an extinct volcano or a volcanic plug. Again, the magma not expelled when the eruption subsided cooled slowly, the presence of conspicuous crystals of white feldspar in the magma distinguished the granite, the rock formed and later cracked into the columns, and over still more time the rest of the volcanic debris and lava eroded away. Heat of

Devil's Tower

summer, cold, rain, and snow of winter continues the erosion to this day, with the exterior granite columns occasionally cracking and crumbling away, though it has been 140 years since the last and only reported instance was witnessed as having occurred.

Whatever story one chooses, the 1,267-foot tower appeared to us suddenly, then disappeared behind trees and hills for several

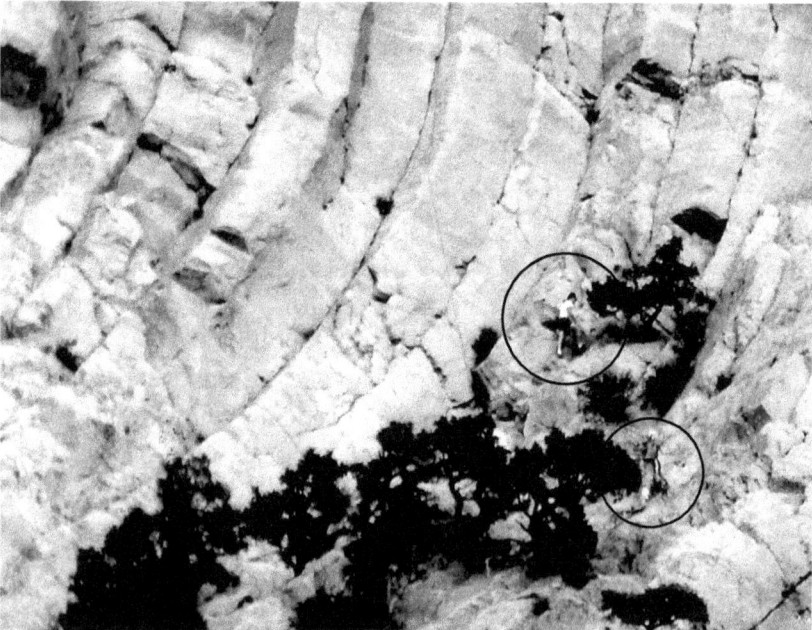
The rock climbers (circled) shows the enormity of the tower.

minutes. It later reappeared again, quintuple sized from the first observation, and it provoked a sense of wonder and awe.

We soon entered the National Monument Park and drove slowly past half-tame prairie dogs in a colony of hundreds. Several who boldly sat by the roadside looking for treats chattered complaint if ignored or noticed too slowly. Up close to the tower, lunch was eaten. Snapping photos as moving clouds passed over the monolith, the colors changed on this massive geological anomaly. Notice was taken that no birds or insects seemed present, and the air was perfectly still and silent. Later, we moved up even closer at the visitor's center area, and watched a team of rock climbers slowly descending, suspended midway down the eight-hundred-foot sheer rock-faced columns.

From the highway, the views of the Wyoming topography grew even more dramatic as the wide-open prairie and sage brush, larger buttes, and huge ridges of six-hundred-foot elevations and higher came into sight and passed on. The term "Rimrock Canyon" took visual form and became a real distinction. Later, back on the Interstate, we chugged our way toward Billings, Montana. As sundown once again filled the windshield, Justin began to doze off. The highway was nearly empty of traffic and false complacency seeped over me.

Out of nowhere, a large western mule-deer appeared in the long shadows, running in the middle of the highway, dead ahead of us. Speed, out in those lonely places, can be deceptive when on a curving downhill run. My glance at the speedometer revealed our velocity at eighty miles per hour! Hitting the brakes as hard as I dared was just enough deceleration to give time for the 160-pound animal to run clear of the pavement and our speeding vehicle.

"Dammit! That was way too close!"

Justin awoke with a start from the evasive maneuvers. I asked, "Did you see that mule deer?"

"Big sucker…stupid deer." he replied with a touch of nonchalance.

My own feelings were far less calm. Any driving drowsiness had been given a shock wake-up call. Impact with such a large animal at that speed would have seriously crushed the entire front end of the car, probably smashed the windshield, and triggered loss of control. Visions of the car plummeting down a two- or three-hundred-foot embankment were not "fun" thoughts. Another potential disaster was averted by a two-second reaction—or less.

Darkness came on before crossing into Montana, and it was fully dark as we traversed through the Crow Indian Reservation and passed by Custer's Last Stand Battleground. Finally rolling into Billings, "No Vacancy" postings greeted us at all the highway motel locations.

"There is a rodeo in town," one of the front desk clerks did say. "Some rooms might be available at one of the hotels downtown."

So onward into the city we proceeded. Passing a dark motel property five minutes later that looked closed, the glow from a television revealed the night clerk in the front office. It was almost midnight.

"Yes, there are rooms available." And at an excellent price. The bed and shower proved welcome relief once again to a long and eventful travel day.

The city of Billings is named after Fredrick H. Billings, President of the Northern Pacific Railroad, which in 1882 built and owned the town. The city has also been known as "Magic City" due to its rapid growth from inception, becoming the largest metro area of the state. Located along the Rimrock Valley of the Yellowstone River, it is astride one of the return passages of the Lewis and Clark Expedition. William Clark had led a small, secondary section of the men to reconnoiter and map the Yellowstone River from its source, while Lewis led the main group back up the Missouri. A bit farther east and by the river is a large monument named Pompey's Pillar, where Clark signed his name in the soft sandstone. This is the only physical evidence remaining of the Expedition passing through the country.

Around Billings are six mountain ranges that were some of the last haunts of the mountain men of story and legend. Comprising the first wave of Americans to invade these Indian lands, the mountain men were seeking riches by trapping lucrative fur animals, particularly beaver. Later, new waves of men joined them to mine precious metals. As the fur industry died out, these frontiersmen also became instrumental as guides of the Emigrant Trails. Easterner "pilgrims" flocked west, seeking to settle in Oregon and California as those territories opened. Historic remnants of wagon train ditches of the Oregon Trail nearby are viewable to this day. The city claims connection to a mountain man personage of historical fame and infamy named John "Liver Eating" Johnston, who acted as deputy sheriff for a short period back in the days of the Wild West.

The Sydney Pollack movie starring Robert Redford as *Jeremiah Johnson* was my first introduction to this character of yesteryear, the movie being a glamorized and toned-down story of the man and his exploits. A more accurate and much more informative source of biography for the arguably most notorious of the mountain men is the book, *Crow Killer* by Raymond W. Thorp and Robert Bunker. Johnston gained notoriety for his "revenge ritual" of cutting out the livers from his hostile Indian victims. He was actually witnessed eating some of the livers, to the insult, dread, and rage of the Indians, and the disgust of civilized whites of that time and now.

Johnston would go on to become one of the most prolific and deadly Indian fighters of the Wild West. It's been said that he once bragged with much satisfaction that for all the killing he had been party to, he'd never taken the life of a child, woman, or white man. Some folks out west feel better about the guy for that, and erected a bronze statue of him in Cody, Wyoming.

Day Five...

As Justin and I departed Billings the next morning, the Rocky Mountains were finally visible. We had been drawing near on the previous day, but they had been obscured by the darkness. To the south stood the eight-thousand-foot tall Pryor Mountains, in easy eyesight across the pure and pristine snow-fed river. Though the posted speed limit was eighty miles per hour, the car felt better running at seventy on the Interstate, and that allowed more comfortable view of the landscape. Soon enough, taller snow-covered peaks could be seen, the Beartooth Range, several exceeding twelve-thousand-foot elevation. Those mountains form a kind of geological northern boundary of the Yellowstone National Park. We had thoughts of routing our trip via a state highway that had been described as the "most beautiful drive in America," to and through the park, but decided our own mountain required first attentions.

We flatlanders proceeded west through what was, for us, a visual paradise as we passed by the rustic-sounding towns and the Crazy Mountains. Those mountains were named after a settler woman who had suffered a mental psychotic break after watching her family killed by Indians, and Johnston's encounter with her is a featured part of the *Jeremiah Johnson* movie, as well as the Johnston biography. Indian legends declare evil spirits reside there and drive people crazy. The winding highway traversed evermore dramatic elevation along the Yellowstone River and the original tracks of the Northern Pacific Railroad, and then veered away for even more serious altitude. Just past noon-time, we had progressed to Livingston, Montana.

"A McDonald's," Justin announced as we spied the familiar golden arches near the approaching exit.

"Civilization at last," he said as I slowed the car, deciding that some gas and food were about due. My child was probably suffering through painful withdrawal while denied that teen food staple for so many days.

We pulled into a combo-station of fuel and food, and decided to split tasks of the stop. Justin would buy Big Macs and fries while I fueled and serviced the car. I pulled up to the food service entrance door, and Justin mentioned he needed access to the trunk to retrieve some of his cash. Hopping out with undisguised glee, he moved behind the car as I remotely unlatched the lock. He began digging through the tightly packed trunk, moving aside items to locate the billfold. I closed my eyes and stretched a bit to relieve the driving tension.

"Dad, we have a problem," Justin called out just a few seconds later. I opened my eyes and looked into the rearview mirror. The trunk lid obstructed a clear view, but as I refocused, I discerned a large amount of dark gray smoke swirling around my son.

"Dad, stop the car and come here! We have a big problem!" Justin shouted, and I turned my head back to get a more direct look. He was now engulfed in a cloud of smoke that was pouring up and out of the entire trunk area.

My God, the car is on fire! My own thoughts shouted as I turned the ignition off, leapt out with rising alarm, and approached this new disaster. Justin was aggressively reaching in at something through the billowing smoke.

"Get back! Don't get burned," I barked while coming into view of the trunk and its contents. "Did you see where the smoke is coming from? Let's move back, back away." I feared the worst, since the gasoline tank was directly below.

"I think I got it," Justin quipped, pointing at a small, smoldering canvas tote bag on the pavement.

I then quickly rifled through the equipment ensconced in the smoke within the trunk myself, pulling backpacks and sleeping bags out onto the pavement while looking for any other possible sources of the smoke. A breeze was gradually clearing the residual vapors. Discovering nothing else burning, I shifted gaze to the still-smoking object on the pavement. After a moment, the smoke emitting from the bag slowed, and I gingerly unzipped it. More smoke puffed out, dissipated, and revealed a large, burnt box of still-smoldering kitchen matches. The fire appeared to have been starved out by lack of oxygen.

The higher altitude and lack of moisture in the air had provided an environment where the slight friction of the matchheads jostling together had caused a spark, and therefore a flash-combustion amongst the other matchheads, all miraculously contained by the bag.

Wow. Another very near miss by the road demons.

Okay! Emergency handled! Justin and I then repacked the trunk and went about the tasks we had assigned ourselves. Gas and oil were serviced to the car, and then we enjoyed feeding our Big Mac attacks. Munching the fast food tradition minutes later did much to ease the high-tension circumstances. There is definitely something very delicious about McDonald's noontime road food. Do they put addictive drugs in that stuff?

The car did restart, albeit reluctantly, so once again we proceeded to ever-higher elevations. The roadside panorama increased in drama, with one view too beautiful and grand to pass by at a rest stop just short of Butte, Montana. Pulling over and parking, photographs were called for, so camera was in hand. There were quite a few fellow travelers at this particular stop, with the parking area nearly full of folks taking photos and walking about. I commented to a fellow traveler walking within earshot, "This is an unusually popular place."

He looked over at us with a knowing smile and responded, "Most of these folks are temporarily stuck here with vehicles that won't start. Ya see, the higher altitude is bad for cars that use premium high octane fuel, which many of the newer, more expensive models require. Lower octane fuel burns best, which is why gas sold in these parts are lower octane grades. But the expensive cars with the new fuel computers don't adapt automatically and stall out. The engines flood with gas by repeated ignition attempts. Most of these folks are waiting for the flooded engines to drain off."

Hmmmm. I looked at the line of very attractive new model vehicles, and the activity around them did seem to verify what this local informant was describing. Our Honda usually burned regular gas, but I had noticed the lower octane readings at our last fill-up, and had used the plus grade when last refueling in Livingston. Were the road demons going to bite at us again?

We moved along to snap a few photos, take advantage of the facilities, and then returned to the car. I turned the ignition. *Va-varrooom*, went my trusty old Honda on the first try.

"I think we just might make it," I spoke aloud for the first time since Sioux Falls, as we pulled out and passed by the line of stalled traveling vehicles.

Justin and I continued to make good time on the Interstate, passing through Butte, picking up I-15 south, and reaching the town of Dewey, Montana. Turning onto a two-lane highway, we followed along the Wise and Big Hole Rivers that sourced farther west. The surrounding timberlands comprised the Beaverhead/ Deerlodge National Forests, with a narrow strip of Montana ranchlands along the roadway, and the snowcapped peaks of the Continental Divide in the distance ahead. At the town of Wisdom, we would link to a road that crossed through the Bitterroot National Forest over to Idaho via the seven-thousand-foot Lost Trail Pass. We descended from the Divide down a heavily wooded western slope that was quite steep and undergoing road construction. Though slowed a bit, the Idaho State Highway ran south unobstructed to and then along the North Fork of the Salmon River. Around five o'clock that evening we rolled into the town of Salmon, the last true civilization before the wilderness. It was easy navigating to a campground near the river at the edge of town, and it fit our needs perfectly. Camping at last!

Both my son and I would become very impressed by the people we met in Salmon; they were most friendly, helpful, and courteous during nearly every interaction. The woman administering the campground was most welcoming while helping us select our campsite, guiding us through the restroom, shower, and laundry facilities, and gracious as we paid the modest camp fee. We were still unloading when a young girl came over from one of the RV sites, surprisingly requesting that she help with the tent set-up, which we allowed. She also promised to "keep-an-eye-out" around our site while we went back to town to find a store. We needed matches.

The young woman attending a small grocery offered us a somewhat resigned, yet the quaintest greeting of our entire journey: "Welcome to The Middle of Nowhere."

Upon return to our camp, we set some charcoal alight, and as it burned down to hot coals, we walked over and chatted with the little girl's folks. They were her grandparents from Bozeman, Montana. Little Trina, age twelve, was vacationing with them on their way to Yellowstone National Park. Trina also volunteered that she "only had one parent"—her father. She added, "My mother doesn't live with me, just my dad does. My mom is crazy." It was clear as I talked with her grandparents, Dorothy and Harold, that they were the parents of her father. Dorothy made a comment, with an amused laugh, that their granddaughter was making big eyes at Justin. Justin was quite polite with the girl as she chatted with him, but shyly paid little heed to her interest. I conversed enjoyably with Trina's grandparents for some ten minutes until the cooking coals were ready, thanked little Trina for her help, then bid adieu to all with everyone grinning.

Proceeding back to our area, we grilled up steak, fried potatoes, and baked beans for dinner—and I enjoyed half a bottle of burgundy wine. We watched the sky turn an idyllic bright gold as dusk followed sundown. Deepening to twilight, the stars came out and the planets brightened. Turning in to our tent with lantern aglow, we updated our journals, played a game of chess, and finally hit lights out for the most satisfied, though not the most restful, sleep of the adventure so far. The ground was still as hard as in my youth, and the ground pads provided only modest comfort.

The Corps of Discovery had passed through this location in late August of 1805 after meeting the Shoshone Indian Tribe. The group of Indians encountered proved to be kinsmen of Sacagawea, the wife of one of the French guides for the river journey, which was most fortunate. Lewis was planning to have these people lead the expedition through the mountains. Having crossed over the

Continental Divide at the Lemhi Pass, farther south than our own crossing, their initial camp was on the Lemhi River, as was ours. That river joined the Salmon River just a few hundred yards from our very campsite.

Historical markers indicated the Corps of Discovery could have slept where we were camping that very night. They would then make their way back north, seeking means of crossing the next mountain range on the other side of the river valley. William Clark had already led a reconnaissance down the Salmon River itself, but reported that the waterway was impassable. Extreme and extended rapids and whitewater made passage too dangerous, fully living up to its Indian name: "The River of No Return."

The Shoshone Indian tribe that had assisted Lewis and Clark during the portage from the Missouri River to the Lemhi River had in fact been already moving to the east for a buffalo hunt. Happenstance was quite lucky that the meeting with the Expedition had occurred at all. Luckier still was that the group initially making contact had been led by Sacagawea's own brother! The tribe was close to starvation, and thus unwilling to continue guiding the Corps of Discovery through the remaining mountain ranges to the west. Since the Salmon River was impassable, the explorers successfully traded white-man manufactured goods, including Lewis's pistol, for twenty-nine cast-off horses in poor condition to continue west. They also did prevail on the Indian chiefs to draft a single, older "volunteer" Indian guide from the tribe to assist them. The two groups then took leave of each other, the American explorers and guide proceeding north along the very highway track Justin and I had traversed into town.

"Lewis assessed the characteristics of the Shoshone (Snake) tribe: 'They seldom correct their children particularly the boys who soon become masters of their own acts. They give as a reason that it cows and breaks the sperit of the boy to whip him, and that he never recovers his independence of mind after he is grown.'"[7]

7 Bergon

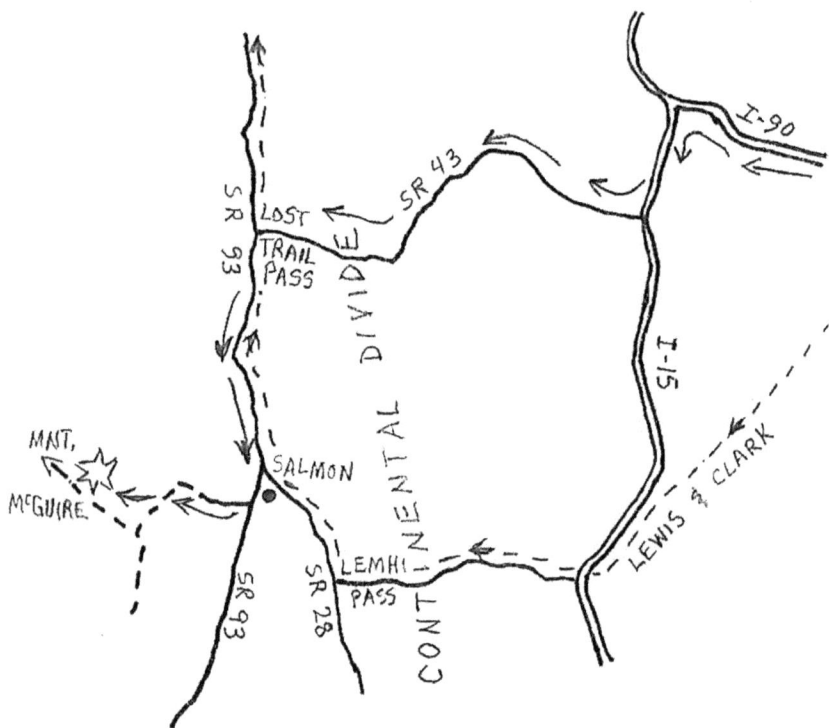

I-90

SR 43

SR 43

SR 93

LOST
TRAIL
PASS

SR 93

I-15

MNT.
McGUIRE

SALMON

LEWIS & CLARK

CONTINENTAL DIVIDE

SR 93

SR 28

LEMHI
PASS

CHAPTER
FOUR

Arising late on day six, the sun was well up in a clear morning sky as Justin and I took a more relaxed and leisurely pace to our start-up activities. We admired the views of the nearby mountain peaks that surround this community. Liberal use of the modern facilities (including the laundry machines), breakfast consumed, camp breakdown, and vehicle repacked were all accomplished by eleven o'clock.

The Forest Service office was the next chosen stop. A sizable single-storied building at the other edge of town housed the district offices of both the U.S. Forestry Service and the U.S. Bureau of Land Management. Parking and entering the lobby, we spied three uniformed rangers at a large reception counter. While walking up, I caught the eye of one, introduced ourselves, and explained where we were from and the objective of our visit.

With a big smile and genuine interest, the ranger assisted us by securing maps and directions to the proper trailhead campsite. He also shared advice about some of the rules and regulations to be observed. Upon our inquiring, he also shared with us the likelihood and kinds of wildlife we might encounter.

"Deer and elk are very common, golden eagles and mountain sheep less so, but the altitude is too high for snakes. Yes, there are mountain lions, but these big cats do all they can to avoid humans. Black bears are out there, too, but there haven't been reports of any 'bear trouble' all year."

"Yes, there was! We had 'bear trouble' two days ago," a woman called out from an office hallway within easy earshot of the reception desk. The woman continued describing a location that I had no familiarity with.

The ranger then turned to us, smiled, and said with confident assurance, "You two are going farther into the forest than the location she's talking about, so you won't have any problems. What are you driving?"

"We have a front-wheel drive Honda Accord. I'm sure we are

good there," I replied with just a touch less confidence, given our recent troubles, and while considering once again the "bear trouble" conversation.

The ranger then took on a more serious tone. "You know that the roads in the mountains are not paved. They are dirt and gravel at best, with lots of debris and deep ruts in places. You might not be able to get to the trailhead. We advise using a four-wheel drive SUV, or at least a full-sized pick-up truck."

"Well, I guess I'll just dump the car there if we get too stuck, since I'm overdue to get a new one," I laughed.

"Don't be leaving your vehicle up there, no, no," he countered me, still quite serious.

"Really, sir, I'm sure we'll make it okay," I answered quickly. "Even if we can't, are there any places close enough along the way to finish by hiking in?" I asked with a respectful humility.

The ranger then relented a bit and obligingly began marking in colored felt-tip pen two places on the mapped roadway that could serve as possible points to park short of the destination. The best was at about three miles, and the second was seven miles out. The seven-mile option didn't sound promising.

I put on my best appreciative face, thanked the ranger profusely for his attentive personal service and help, and followed with one last inquiry: "Grizzly bears?"

"Grizzly bears are over on the other side of the mountains in Yellowstone, up in Glacier, and Canada, but we don't have them in this area," he answered with continuing reassurance. "Good luck, and have a great trip," he finished with another smile.

We thanked him again while turning to leave. As Justin and I returned to our vehicle, a question I silently pondered was, *how is it that being deeper in the wilderness reduces risk of 'bear trouble'?*

Upon our return to the town center and a local sporting outfitter shop, we purchased another couple of camp items, fishing licenses, and bait. With all the lakes in the area, my thought was to try some fishing, using the two compact fishing poles and reels I'd purchased back home. A grocery stop followed to gather some fresh foods for our time up in the mountains, but as we walked back out to the parking lot, it began to rain. It was nearly three o'clock by now, and our information was that the mountain trailhead campground was another three to five hour's driving time away, depending on my car's performance.

With the specter of the road potentially becoming impassible, and possibly having to backpack an extra three to seven miles, starting that late in the day would risk darkness arriving well before reaching the campground up there. Hiking in rain to a place we had not been to before and lugging all our accouterment through obviously steep, rugged terrain was clearly beyond our inexperienced capabilities. Justin agreed it was a good idea to delay for an extra night, so we returned to our previous camping spot as rain and wind began intensifying.

Our tent was raised before the rain became soaking, and we retreated to the Honda as wind and a downpour ensued. While sitting the storm out, a sudden wind shear flipped the awning of a neighboring fifth-wheel trailer up and onto the RV's roof. Not five minutes later, the owner returned, got out of his truck, and attempted to wrestle the awning back into place with futility, against the wind and rain.

I woke my dozing son by saying, "Time for a good deed. Let's go." *A Scout is helpful*. We exited the car and trotted over to lend a needed hand to our neighbor's predicament. Good fortune followed immediately when both wind and rain slowed and another fellow camper arrived. We all working together quickly, removed the damaged awning, and patched the roof. As Justin and I started to return to our own site, our new neighbor, Tom, invited us back over for a beer and some conversation.

Tom was one of the more interesting people we met on the trip. A professor of sociology on a six-month research sabbatical from University of Kentucky, he was traveling all over the West. His subject concerned the long-standing anti-Federal Government political views held by many folks living in the western states and their cultural impact on the country and politics. Involved was the interviewing of individuals from diversified occupations, educations, incomes, wealth, religious affiliations, locations, and lengths of residency.

At some point, he divulged to being single and traveling alone, thus no broken heart had been left behind. Tom welcomed some light diversion.

When I mentioned that what he was doing sounded like the coolest job in the world, he laughed. He then half-seriously, if not more, encouraged me to consider going back to school at age forty-four. "Lots of older people are going back."

It was my turn to laugh and respond, "Perhaps I'll give it consideration after Justin has his first run at it."

We talked for about an hour, our new friend proving to be a wealth of informative conversation on a wide range of topics. He was well versed in history, science, world politics, and kept his words and educated insights simple, yet engaging. Tom also listened very well. We concluded when the rain finally stopped, which was also when the beer did. Justin and I then took our leave.

We opted to eat dinner at a restaurant back in the town center rather than practice camp cooking in the wet. The town diner served a fairly wide variety of excellent menu choices, and the meals were well prepared, economically priced, and tasted most satisfactory. The movie *Twister* was playing at the main-street movie house just a block away, so we took in that entertainment as well. The film seemed a coincidental and apt dramatization for how our vacation had unfolded just three days prior, with a second reminder that very day.

It was good that we delayed and relaxed an extra night. Fatigue can sneak up on you and adrenalin can only compensate for a while before long-term tiredness begins to overwhelm. Judgement gets clouded and good decision making is impaired. Reactionary actions become ineffective or even counterproductive. The delays caused by the late start, car breakdown, continued vehicle vulnerabilities, and questions of its reliability had compelled me to assume all driving. I had been pushing a little more each of the preceding six days. But, like Meriwether Lewis at nearly the same point of his journey two hundred years earlier, I was determined to get over all obstacles—come hell or high water—and get us within sight of our mountain.

***

Bear, as a word, has at least twenty-eight definitions in the English dictionary. Our road trip had used several as a verb thus far: to support or hold up; to bring or convey; to tolerate or endure; to move, be located, or to lie in a specific direction. My own life experience had several exposures to some of the noun definitions lower down on the list. Working as a stock broker, I'd speculated selling short, being a "bear" as an investor in anticipation of clawing down to lower prices. Socially, I had dealt with an ill-mannered or irritating bear of a person. But it was the first noun definition that was issuing the most sizzle during this trip, aside from seeing our mountain itself:

Any plantigrade mammal of the family Ursidae: order Carnivora (carnivores). Bears are typically massive omnivorous animals with a large head, a long shaggy coat, and strong claws. [8]

The average size of black bears in the Northwestern Rockies is reported as 148 pounds for females and 262 pounds for males. The estimated population of black bears nation-wide is around six-hundred thousand. Reports of black bears of 350 to 400 pounds are more than occasional.

The National Park Service issues the following on their webpage immediately after the topic black bears:

"Warning: Bears are wild animals that are dangerous and unpredictable. Do not approach bears or allow them to approach you! Do not feed bears! ...Use binoculars, telephoto lens, or a spotting scope to view the animals."

Further instructions follow:

"Although extremely rare, attacks on humans have occurred, inflicting serious injuries and death. If you see a bear remain watchful.
Don't run...Try to increase distance between you and the bear. If a bear persistently follows or approaches you, stand your ground and shout *(harsh language?)* at the bear, throw rocks and have a big stick...
If the bear shows no interest in your food and you're physically attacked, fight back aggressively with any available object—the bear may consider you as prey!
Report all bear incidents to a park ranger immediately...
Help protect others."

Even though the number of fatal black bear attacks in the wild of North America within my lifetime had been reported as a very small handful, the serious injury statistic is significant enough. That statistic about being mauled and maimed...you know the one...scarred for life with half a face, for instance...or missing an arm or a leg...

8 Merriam-Webster Dictionary

By all official reports, there would be no grizzly bears in our area, but with one caveat not obvious in the publications and reporting—grizzly bears are a solitary being and roam widely. The isolated population in Yellowstone ranges outward 250 miles into the surrounding, sparsely human-inhabited mountain and forest areas. That wider range serves to connect Yellowstone grizzly populations to those larger bear populations in Glacier National Park and Canada. In fact, isolated sightings, albeit most unofficial, have been reported up and down the Continental Divide in the lower forty-eight states from New Mexico to Washington State. The spine of the Rocky Mountains acts as a last refuge and the migration path connecting the bear populations all the way to Alaska.

The word "grizzly" was first coined by American naturalist George Ord in 1815. Ord also classified the bear for its character, "Ursus horribilis," and this varmint well deserves the name. American Indian tribes setting out to hunt these bears conducted the same pre-hunt rituals as when going to war.

Meriwether Lewis recorded his first encounters with this beast in 1805, who resides at the top of the North American animal food chain:

"On April 29, Lewis was walking on shore with one of [his men] when they spotted two grizzlies. Each man fired and hit a bear. One of the wounded beasts escaped, but the other charged Lewis, pursuing him some eighty yards. Fortunately, the bear was badly enough wounded that Lewis [and his companion] had time to reload. They shot again and killed it. Though not full grown, it weighed three hundred pounds. Lewis described it as a 'much more furious and formidable animal' than the black bear of the eastern United States. 'It is astonishing to see the wounds they will bear before they can be put to death,' he admitted but remained cocky: the Indians 'may well fear the anamal... but in the hands of skilled riflemen [the bears] are by no means as formidable or dangerous' as the Indians indicated...

On May 5, his cockiness began to fade. Clark and Drouillard [a civilian guide and interpreter] killed a grizzly. Lewis described it as, 'a most tremendious looking anamal, and extreemly hard to kill notwithstanding he had five balls through his lungs and five others in various parts he swam more than half the distance across the river to a sandbar & it was twenty minutes before he died; [he] made the most tremendous roaring from the moment he was shot.' Clark estimated the bear's size to be 500 lbs. while Lewis thought it more like 600 lbs. On May 11, after yet another grizzly bear encounter, Lewis writes in conclusion, 'these bears being so hard to die reather intimedates us all; I must confess that I do not like the gentlemen and had reather fight two Indians than one bear.'" [9]

The American grizzly bear's average standing height is six-and-a-half feet tall, average weight is three hundred pounds for an inland female, and six hundred pounds for an inland male. Some grizzly bears on the Pacific coast have exceeded ten feet tall, five feet wide at the shoulders, and 1,500 pounds in weight. Most human fatalities in the wild occur by females protecting their cubs or from aggressive males during mating season, that season running from May through July. Or, if the bear is hungry and decides you are the prey. Recent estimates put the grizzly bear population in North America at about fifty-five thousand. They account for more than twice as many fatal attacks on humans in the wild than the black bear. This is still only a very small fraction of the fatal hunting accidents involving firearms each year.

9 Ambrose

Mountain sides and perilous roads

CHAPTER FIVE

Day Seven, Evening ...

Journal entry:

Despite all warnings and mini-disasters, Justin and I are camping at the Crags trailhead campground, 8,470 ft. up one of the most harrowing (and scary) roads I've ever seen. HondaCar got his bottom hard scraped a couple of times, but chugged up and over every hurdle. The rocks and ruts were as advertised, but we were lucky and very cautious. They said it would take two-and-a-half hours, but we took it slower—about 4 hours and 15 minutes. It's a lot cooler here, particularly at night. It is raining and finally dark at 10 P.M. Justin is asleep, worn out from the day's journey. He didn't do any sleeping in the car today.

As I write this, I find myself imagining bears and other critters sniffing us out since I have the tent closed up and can't see outside. This campground has a resident Forest Service person and about 7 other campers widely dispersed. There is tap water, but it's not turned on, so they don't charge any camp fee yet. Talked to the resident, a second forest ranger, and a local outfitter/guide as we rolled in—they were testing the water for any contaminants, particularly Giardia, from a tank they have set up. So, we will be borrowing drinking water for the next couple of days—they say it takes that long for the test results. We are camped along a mountain stream with water so pure looking, but we have to use purifier tablets or boil it before drinking—we just use it for cooking & cleaning. I have noticed a shortness of breath and will be acclimating myself up here before attempting any hiking. But Mount McGuire is only 10 miles away, and Justin is eager to attempt it. We also brought fishing gear and will try that too until we break it.

Am now going to smoke my last cigarette.

Giardia, short for *Giardia lamblia*, is a flagellated protozoan parasite that is one nasty bug to become infected with. Giardia infects humans, cats, dogs, birds, cattle, beavers, deer, and sheep through ingestion of dormant microbial cysts in contaminated water, or by the fecal-oral route through bad personal hygiene. The cyst can survive for weeks or months in cold water occurring in natural ponds, wells, and clean-appearing mountain streams, and is resistant to conventional treatment such as chlorination. After ingestion, the bug colonizes in the small intestine, and fifty percent of the time manifests symptoms in humans of diarrhea, malaise, excessive gas, and foul or sulfuric-tasting belching, which is known to be so nauseating in taste that it induces violent vomiting. Other symptoms are pale, foul-smelling, and greasy stools, epigastric pain, bloating, general nausea, diminished interest in food, and weight loss.

The conventional treatments have side-effects, including metallic taste, diarrhea, vomiting, dizziness, headache, increased risk of other infections, hair loss, and drowsiness. Treatments vary from one to seven days. Full recovery can often take weeks or even months. Some may recall a top NFL football player contracting Giardia by drinking untreated water from a "crystal-clear mountain stream" while on a hunting trip in Montana. His recovery lasted six months or more, and his short career was cut shorter, ending within three years...all ruined by drinking water that some animal upstream had crapped in. Experts advise that boiling the water for a minute or more is the surest method of making the water safe to drink. [10]

***

Day seven started with an early, partly-cloudy sky. The intermittent sun was interpreted as a good omen. On the road by eleven o'clock, we followed the highway south out of town for five miles and crossed the Main Salmon River due west for another three miles of pavement. The road turned to gravel just before the entrance sign to the Salmon National Forest, where the byway remained two lanes wide as we climbed up the first switchback. Though the posted speed said thirty miles per hour, I had reduced our speed to the twenties and was already avoiding loose, sharp-

10 www.healthline.com

edged gravel rocks known to cut and puncture even multi-ply tires. The first hurdle was one third of the way, some vertical six hundred feet up the switchback, where a road construction crew was at work installing road drainage wedges and large concrete blocks to act as guard rails. Long, fifteen-inch-high furls of soft dirt crisscrossed the turn and driving surface upward, which threatened to trap our vehicle. A highly-revved engine and the front-wheel drive proved just sufficient enough to fishtail up and through, with the furled dirt scraping the bottom of the car. As we drove past, a very skeptical-looking road crew watched us go onward up the first mountainside.

The altitude we'd started at was about four thousand feet above sea level, so Justin and I were at nearly five times the altitude of our hometown. That ascent had been gradual over six days, whereas on this day we would more than double that in just a few hours. Continuing ever higher through this mountain passageway, the top was reached about one hour into the drive. The path we were traversing was a logging road. We were then in the midst of descending another mountain switchback, the road winding in and out of the mountain spurs with plenty of blind turns.

Suddenly, a huge semi-truck with a log-loaded trailer charged at us from a blindsided curve on the left-inside track, plus occupying our half of any middle of the graveled surface. While Justin and I held our breath, I eased the car over as far as I dared to the edge and stopped, where a slight pullover space gave a last-second opportunity to avoid head-on collision. No guardrail between us and a 1,500-foot drop to the valley below offered solace. The road monster blew by within inches without slowing his full acceleration, throwing up a fistful of bouncing gravel, which rattled against the car while covering us with thick brown dust. *She-e-e-e-t!* Really, really close!

Despite the road monster scare, the valley we were entering was one of the most dramatically beautiful we had seen that far on our trip. The gravel road visibly looped ever downward like stepping stone slabs through the forested slope of the mountainside. Once reaching the valley floor, Panther Creek rushed by the road's edge with dark blue, crystal-clear snowmelt water punctuated with thousands of whitecaps. Following the road signage gave us clear direction, and soon we were passing the town of Cobalt, Idaho, population: one.

Though there was only one full-time resident, the town contained two or three cottages, a mini-motel/meeting house complex, and several house trailers and RVs were sited and parked along the creek and a field area amongst scattered trees. This was a sizable trout fly-fishing resort during the warm summers, and the temporary population could expand to well over a hundred people on any given week of the season. The single full-time resident owned a ranch comprising a large portion of the valley area, with a small herd of horses and cattle. An impressive log ranch house of modern design gave the homestead postcard-perfect character. Not bad digs for a person who served as the town postmaster.

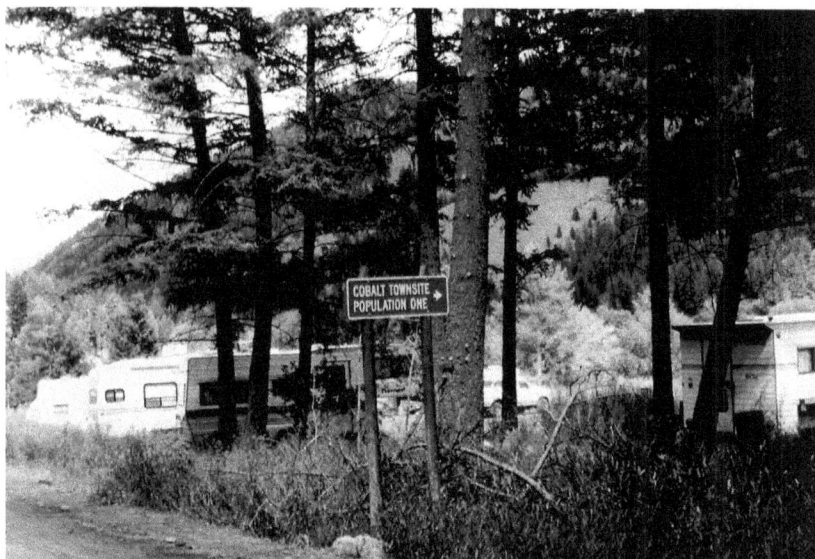

Cobalt, ID

The road split at the edge of town, one way veering right to Blackbird Mountain and a possibly operating gold mine, said a sign. To the left, following the creek, were the Bighorn Crags and our destination. We passed a ranger station with several buildings, vehicles, and a helicopter pad about two miles later, near a small State Park on the creek. Not long after those landmarks, we turned at a sign leading up another mountain. This single-lane track quickly degenerated into a sometimes rough, dynamite-blasted surface with gravel filling in the holes, or at least most of them, at first.

At several spots where the grade was particularly steep, ruts and large rocks combined with serious erosion troughs that destroyed any semblance of the road being horizontally level, and our vehicle tilted to the side by twenty degrees at times. The car couldn't average even ten miles per hour. Far less was dared as we weaved around the extreme spots, stopped to move rocks too large to evade or pass over, and sloshed through mini-streams several inches wide and deep from the snow melt.

Occasionally looking over the roadside cliffs at wild and grand mountain views inspired us forward despite the treacherous road conditions, until over one last crest was revealed the panorama of the Crags. We were very much relieved after such an ascent as we eased downward and into a forested campground, and pulled up to three men engaged in conversation. Two donned ranger uniforms and were standing under the trees.

"Which one of you guys is in charge of that road up to here? That's the worst road I've ever seen, even in the movies. Somebody ought to think about fixing that thing," I said to open my own conversation, smiling—yet quite serious.

One uniformed ranger, a slender man of average height and in his late forties, stepped forward. Answering with unapologetic candor and a grin, he said, "Well, you can have this place all to yourself, pristine and pure, or you can have half the fruits and nuts from California up here with you. Who told you that little car was a good idea? Most folks use at least a full-sized truck comin' up here. Surprised ya made it at all."

"Good point," I laughed while shaking his hand. We exchanged introductions.

They were genuinely pleased to hear of our endeavor, and Roy, the trailhead campground resident, also in uniform, directed us to what he considered a great campsite to set ourselves up in. He stated we were in one of the most amazing and beautiful spots in the country, second to none, and he would check in with us later, once we got settled in.

"But don't drink the camp spigot water because it still has bacteria in it, and there will be no charged camp fee until it is potable." He offered sharing some of his own water with us. That was a great offer, because purifier tablets give water a nasty metallic taste, and boiling it would take a lot of extra time when our own three gallons of fresh water ran out. Even though there were residual patches of snow on the ground, pristine it no longer looked. The "clear" appearing stream beside our site would be used for washing only. With our thanks, he departed and left us to our campsite set-up.

"Alacrity" would've described our practiced movements as we raised the tent, a dining fly, and had a nice fire started within the hour. Dinner followed soon after. It had been darkening overcast since driving up the last mountain, and a light sprinkle of rain had intermittently fallen since our arrival. But cold rain mist and the low fifty-degree temperature did little to discourage a growing hoard of mosquitos that forced us to move our dinner inside the tent. After dinner and clean-up, Justin and I played cards for a half hour or so, but the continued falling temperatures ended shared activities, save my recreational reading and journal update. Sleeping didn't come soon in my case.

Tossing back and forth, I found little solace in a remedy I had acquired for my paranoia and fears of what might lurk in the dark. That remedy was my having broken down and purchasing a firearm. Touching and holding the handgun I had finally acquired as last resort personal protection only reminded me of awful choices I did not want to be forced to make. Sleep, when it did finally come, was interrupted frequently by the temperature plummeting further still, and exacerbated by at least three urgent trips outside the tent to urinate with flashlight in hand as steady rain showered down.

Standing vulnerable, shivering, I flashed the light beam one way, then another, nervously seeking what might hide and stalk in the dark shadows. "Sweet Jesus." Dorothy was back in my head with fears of the lurking wolves, lions, and bears, (Oh, my!) I was seven years old again.

The campground had lots of deadfall timber lying in rows, reminiscent of several hunting and wildlife videos I'd seen in the past. Footage had shown bears looking up and approaching the camera with menace.

I shuddered and relieved myself next to the tree a few paces from the tent. The exercise proved an absurdity, as I found it impossible to juggle the flashlight, the cold steel of the pistol, and my shriveled pecker with just two hands. The pistol proved one item too many as I fumbled about in the cold and freezing rain while tending to my urgent business.

I ultimately forgot and/or deliberately left the weapon in the tent after the first bladder relief run.

***

Few gun owners have likely suffered the deliberative process I inflicted upon myself when deciding to purchase a firearm. Though I had some very limited experience with the .22 caliber target rifle in my teen Boy Scout years and had fired a friend's .38 revolver at a target range once, my household was one where firearms were absent, both as a boy and as an adult. More than once I'd considered buying a gun, but usually only when I was angry with someone who had intimidated me, which my values dictated was the worst of reasons—to my mind, a clear overreaction to adolescent immaturity, and a sure sign of character weakness. I had little need of such a possession for work nor interest in any recreational aspect.

Emotional issues also were a big consideration, as well as accidental injury statistics. All of these factors implied owning firearms might not be my best idea. But the weight of my friends' arguments regarding safety in the wilderness for my son had altered the paradigm.

Quite a few of my friends owned firearms of all sorts, and several weeks of conversations with them did enlighten many aspects of the topic. After more authoritative research and study, I took personal inventory of what attributes were most important to me in such an item. Some sort of handgun became the focus. Ease of handling, simplicity of operation and carry seemed like good attributes, and the popular Glock 9mm automatic received the most votes from my sources. The qualifications and validity of my personal sources were suspect, however, given that they were a bunch of guys at a local diner I frequented.

The gun dealer I found myself in front of, referred by one of the self-described "diner counter-trash crowd," presented new clarity on this personal protection matter: "Yeah, the Glock will be fine, even preferable against a mountain lion, wolf, or small bear, but if you come up against a larger black bear or grizzly, all you're gonna do is piss him off. Even firing the full clip, it'll still charge and kill ya for certain. Ya need a .44 Magnum to handle the Grizzly, for sure." He pulled a large revolver from the display case and handed it to me.

The weapon seemed huge, with a six-inch barrel and heavy bulk to absorb the recoil of its large-caliber, high-velocity projectile. "Ya need a bullet with magnum-charged velocity to penetrate the hide and muscle of the grizzly, to hit the heart, because they don't scare by just being wounded. They get mad and keep coming, so that there is your best option," the gun dealer continued while I held what felt like a small cannon.

"What about the .357 Magnum?" I inquired, spying a smaller handgun in the display case with a competent-looking "Police" label.

"That gun might also do the trick, since the projectile velocity is even higher, but the slug is smaller," while trading me this second product to hold.

One of my friends had a similar firearm and bragged about its power and accuracy. Holding the alternative weapon with a four-inch barrel, it still seemed far larger than I felt comfortable with. As I mentioned that to the gun dealer, he reached into the display case and handed me option number three: a .357 Magnum Double-Action, five-shot revolver with a two-inch barrel. This pistol was clearly smaller and lighter in weight.

When I asked about the recoil, he smiled and said, "I carry this particular pistol myself. The difference in recoil is minimal with the Smith & Wesson. Accuracy is the only drawback of a shorter barrel, so if you are confronted, you should wait until a bear target is within twenty feet, and ten is better. If it's a grizzly, the head is your best killing shot if you can shoot the skull direct-on through the mouth or the top of the head. But most of all, you must be comfortable with the firearm."

Since shooting a protected species was a last-resort option, my simple logic confirmed that the animal must be very close before I would feel compelled to use this weapon. The man made sense. The weapon seemed to best meet my criteria, and "last resort" purpose. Without much further discussion, the purchase was made, and at quite a lower cost than I had expected to spend on this precautionary insurance. Hook, line, and sinker, I had swallowed the dealer's sales pitch.

George, the coffee-counter friend, who had accompanied and introduced me to this gun dealer, also agreed that what the man said made sense. Another validation came from Jim, my roommate, whom I enlisted to help me test the firearm. It was the same weapon he carried himself at work as a private security guard. He was excited to accompany me to the range, since he had never actually practice-fired his own pistol yet.

We met at a local private shooting range the next day, purchased target ammo and ear plugs, and rented goggles and an hour of range time. Jim volunteered to go second, so I lined up the target from twenty feet distance away, and took two-handed aim at dead center on the silhouette. Tightening my grip, my thumb pulled back the trigger-hammer until it cocked, and then I slowly squeezed the trigger. The simultaneous explosion of the magnum load and near-blinding flash emitting from the barrel was shocking. The recoil was stronger than advertised. But this first single discharge of the handgun put to rest any qualms regarding the weapon's power. My target-shooting partner was all smiles as I exclaimed, "Wow!"

The following four shots were carefully fired in like fashion, and we pulled the target in to see my score. All five bullet slugs had hit the silhouette, all but one within the most center ring. Another firing round followed where I sped up my rate of discharging the pistol—five shots in fifteen seconds. I continued my practice, dispensing with cocking the weapon and firing simply by pulling the trigger. Variations employed were of more rapid firing, longer distance, and use of my left hand. My scores declined each round. I then declared myself done. The base of my thumb was swollen double sized and aching. Later practices did accomplish more comfort with the handling of the pistol, as I adjusted to its weight, sound, and recoil, though the target scores improved not at all.

"Confidence is the key," goes the conventional wisdom….and such does delusional thinking begin…a common side-effect of adopting and believing the BS of others.

Day Eight…

Day two in the mountains began at six o'clock in the morning. The temperature was around freezing, as indicated by the ice on the surface of the cup of water containing my final cigarette butt from the night before. We awoke with runny noses, headaches, and head congestion that is symptomatic of acclimating abruptly to high altitude. Emerging from our sleeping bags, the air revealed frosty breath. Quickly dressed, we vacated the tent for yet another restroom trip, this time walking about seventy-five meters to the sheltered campground pit toilet. Upon return, shivers from the damp, penetrating, and freezing cold added urgency to build a fire—pronto. Nothing quite measures up to a warming early morning campfire in any outdoor circumstance, but in this instance, "Salvation from suffering," best described our urgency.

Woodcraft defined, as referred to in Scouting, are the skills and experience in matters relating to living and thriving in the woods, such as hunting, fishing, and camping on a short- or long-term basis. Recreational woodcraft might include knowledge of wildlife behaviors, identifying wild plants and animals for cooking, orienteering with the stars and sun, using a map and compass, hiking techniques, fire making, use of ropes, lashings, and knots, tents, and wilderness first aid. Most of these skills are derived from American Indian woodlore. Woodlore skills of the Native American Indians were a necessary education for European colonists for them to explore and survive independently in the wilderness of North America. Frontiersmen such as Daniel Boone, Kit Carson, and the mountain men learned and used these skills as they spearheaded the westward exploration, conquest, and expansion of white settlement. This guaranteed U.S. dominion over lands coveted by the European colonial powers of Spain, France, Russia, and Britain.

Frederick Burnham learned these skills through a series of experienced mentors and the Indians. *"His father had been known as a Kentucky frontiersman and rifle-shooting parson who could bark a squirrel, swing an ax, or dispense the Gospel with equal fervor and efficiency."*[11] Thus, Reverend Edwin Burnham was Frederick's first mentor as a boy, and he taught him the frontier skills of that time: riding, shooting, hunting, and woodlore. Fred was already well trained enough that the eleven-year-old boy had scouted and learned the Los Angeles area during the two years before his father's passing. The young lad secured a job when his mother and little brother moved back east with the Western Union office as a messenger. Fending for himself, he hunted game in the area with a rifle of his own purchase. Burnham conducted his "graduate work" of mastering the arts of scouting, tracking, and outdoor survival skills in the late 1870s and early 1880s. Frederick participated with U.S. military expeditions to hunt down Geronimo

11 Lott, Jack

in the Apache Wars. He served as an army scout and Indian tracker with the old army veterans, frontier trailblazers, and mountain men, who, with white settlement and civilization steadily advancing, turned to scouting for army detachments sent to pacify the Arizona Territory. These older, grizzled experts at the closing days of their years often wanted to impart to a younger generation their own hard-earned knowledge and lore of the frontier.

One older mentor named Holmes, who had served with Kit Carson and John C. Fremont, befriended and partnered with Fredrick. He taught the teen how to properly ascend and descend precipices, tell time at night, protect himself from snakes, and find water in all types of terrain. It was all about the details of simple things, such as how to braid rope, tie a knot, and the proper way to build a fire using minimum natural elements without matches. In addition to the army scouting, the two earned a living by hunting, prospecting, working as guides, guarding the mines in the area, and being cowboys.

***

Upon reflection, it was my mother who most facilitated my love of the great outdoors. The fact that Mom was from a rural, agricultural village provided a rich venue for childhood game experiences and a sometimes-overactive imagination. Farm fields, pastureland, as well as sizable wooded areas enhanced realism to the playing stage, where a kid could emulate heroic characters of exploration and frontier history as depicted in books and on television shows. Regular visits to see my grandparents and other relatives there provided the bonus of plenty of like-aged cousins and friends to join in the fun. Lots of trees, hills, and even a flowing creek full of tad poles, salamanders, and an occasional minnow fish, lent "wilderness" to the scene. Best of all was that seasons of the year rarely restricted these games. Not sun, rain, or cold obstructed play, and often offered new dimension. Loose adult supervision, the camaraderie of peers, and few restrictions by formal abstract rules were a taste of freedom that became my addiction. A nearby park in the city and an undeveloped area in the neighborhood provided additional opportunities for this indulgence.

Participation in Scouting added organization and real skillsets that transformed a child's imaginary game to a favored recreation.

Mother was my most influential enabler, fully supporting my joining a Scout Troop at age eleven. It was Mom who took me shopping for the uniform, sewed on the patches, and assisted in selection of the needed equipment and implements. She supported my perseverance with the program when set-backs occurred, and taught me the all-important skills of cooking. She supervised many a lesson of food preparation for our family meals prior to my required test demonstrations of competency. Cooking meals for a family of nine was good practice.

The Scouting Troop I first joined comprised about twenty boys, one being an Eagle, an experienced Scoutmaster, and five or six assisting adults. It was sponsored by our parish church and the meetings were on Friday nights. The scheduled spring camp outing the very next weekend offered immediate participation with the core of the outdoor programs. I learned to properly pitch a tent, tie new rope knots, and cook on a fire without using utensils.

Supposedly, one can cook a burger patty by wrapping it in large, fresh green leaves of a tree or bush, and setting it right on the coals of a campfire. But my burger got pretty charred when the leaves caught fire around the edges. It had plenty of "natural herbs and spices" that tasted just like ashes! I earned the rank of Tenderfoot and decided cooking food with utensils is always easier—and tastes better.

Another lesson absorbed was that snakes are not all bad, but the worst ones are sneaky. Aside from my fears of one entering our tent to curl up next to a warm body, a new caution was added. Copperhead snakes wait aside hiking trails silently, and if spooked by the unwary, they will strike a viciously venomous bite. Our afternoon day hike within the State Park encountered such a specimen, and required a roundabout detour off the trail to avoid the varmint. Despite the good outcome, I still have snake nightmares.

Fortuitously, one of Dad's childhood best friends, Bates A., was a member of our church, and agreed to become the new Scoutmaster the following year. Bates' son, Mark, who was a year older than I, was also a fledgling member of the Troop. The new Troop Leader was not as well versed on Scoutcraft skills as the previous leader had been, but his unfamiliarity did not reduce his enthusiasm. Though there were no senior Scouts left in the Troop, and none of the remaining assisting adults had much prior Scouting experience, Mr. A. did his very best. He was highly committed to our having a good time.

There were four formal Troop outings that year, and on two of the camping events, my dad attended. The spring overnight campout was most notable. It rained buckets as we hiked in with our equipment on a Friday evening. The location was quite wooded, but a small open area provided a perfect, albeit soggy, place to set up camp. I achieved quite a bit of recognition for being the only Scout able to start a campfire that night and the following morning, in the continuing, though thankfully intermittent, rain.

From study of the Scout manual, memory reminded that one can find dry wood, even in the rain, on the side of a tree opposite from the direction that the wind is driving the rain toward. Usually, this will be on the north side of the tree where a moss often grows. By scouting around the woods and identifying the side of the trees with moss, several dead, dry branches, called squaw wood, were found. The dry and quite combustible twigs and branches were harvested. With two matches, ignition was achieved, and the small stick kindling also burned well. Once the fire had built up enough flame and heat, the larger but damper wood burned quite nicely. Repeating the process the next morning enabled cooking a fine breakfast of eggs, sausage, and toast for the Scoutmaster and another attending adult. This feat qualified as a pass for the 2nd Class Scout cooking requirement.

The Scoutmaster's son prepared breakfast for my dad. Mark's ambition was bacon and pancakes, but he probably didn't get the coaching from his mother that I had from my own. He gave it his all, but the outcome wasn't particularly appetizing. The bacon caught fire in the pan and burnt to a crisp and his campfire expired while the pancakes were cooking. The extra time required to rekindle his fire didn't help the pancakes cook through adequately without their burning black first. The comparative outcomes were quite the joke between Mr. A. and my dad. My Scoutmaster declared he got the best deal. Overcoming adversities and discomforts while performing the sometimes-daunting tasks of the outdoors successfully, with praise, is always sweet.

The adult leadership of the Troop changed again over the following summer, and only two outdoor events were successfully scheduled the following year. The biweekly meetings were less well organized and not regularly attended either. By springtime, the Troop folded up altogether due to lack of adult leadership and Scout members' participation. My slow advancement in Scout skill requirements over those two years were also uninspiring. Though a Patrol Leader, which did much to maintain my enthusiasm, I'd only advanced to the 2nd Class Scout Rank.

Since my son missed the Boy Scouting experience, my plan was to mentor Justin myself, sharing my Scoutcraft knowledge and teach him the wood lore skills I knew well. I used this fire-building task to instruct Justin about the three distinctions of wood fuel that, if used correctly, would work every time. Crafting a small blaze using a single match with very small twigs of dry tinder, I added dry, smaller sticks as kindling and larger sticks to fuel a sizable fire within minutes. Use of the match was cheating a little. Employing the more authentic but cumbersome methods of either "flint and steel" or "fire by wood friction" would require more time and prior preparations. We wanted fire fast, and fast it was.

We alternated sitting and standing close to the fire, moving every couple of minutes to avoid the smoke that pursued us. Other damp wood fuel that we added generated nearly as much smoke as heat. The campground was thickly treed, a canopy shading the entire area. A darkly overcast sky completely blocked evidence of the sun's location, and the gray morning twilight lingered. Bright flames warmed bodies and spirits as the dawn did slowly brighten the day. By eight-thirty, it was light enough to qualify as a gloomy, wet morning. My vow to quit smoking and its accompanying nicotine withdrawal agitated me to start cooking up some campfire breakfast.

The plan was to prepare eggs, bacon, and pancakes, but this highlighted the need to repair our initial camp setup. The rain and wind had collapsed half of the dining rain-fly, and the part that still stood hid pockets of rainwater. Cold water drenched me each time I walked near the picnic table. Of course, nearly every implement needed for the task had been placed on the picnic table. Caffeine deprived, a brain-fog allowed concentration on one thought at a time only. The vow to also quit caffeine had my thinking and all movement coordination retarded. Another impediment to the task was the fatigue of the high-altitude acclimation after even modest exertions.

In Scouts, I had learned a lot about cooking outdoors, including menu planning, fire-craft, cooking methods, and sanitation. I hoped to demonstrate the proper methods and skills to my son such that, on the morrow, it would be he who tried his hand at cooking breakfast. But my show was awkward and felt like slow motion. Nicotine withdrawal triggered impatience and frustrations that my harsh language did not help. Once finally prepared, the food did much to soften my agitations. Afterward, we napped for a couple of hours into the afternoon, totally fatigued from the morning exertions and much-interrupted slumbers of the night before.

Roy, the campground resident, came by shortly after we had risen and eaten some lunch. He was delivering five gallons of water, far more than we had expected. Chatting a bit about the wilderness, he described what animals we were likely to see and what to do if lost. He added a few more wilderness tips I hadn't heard of before, and advised about preparations. He also inquired about our outdoor experience.

Justin manning the campfire

"I was in Boy Scouts as a kid, and did lots of hiking and camping while earning the Eagle Scout rank," was my volunteered answer. "You won't have worries with us on that count. And, my golden rule is to always leave the outdoors better than you found it."

"That will work just fine," Roy laughed. "You're going to love this place as much as I do, for certain."

Scouting has the following oath regarding behavior while engaged in the outdoors:

I will do my best to –
        Be clean in outdoor manners.
        Be careful with fire.
        Be considerate in the outdoors.
        Be conservation minded.

The Big Horn Crags Vicinity Map

Roy was a retired gentleman from Texas and had been coming to this trailhead as the Forest Service Summer Resident for five years. He was very affable and good natured.

"I've hiked all of the trails, and even blazed a few of my own. There is lots of beauty out there," he said with a tone of reminiscent pleasure.

Continuing after a long pause, "You know, this entire campground was under six feet of snow just two weeks ago, and that road you drove up here on was under ten feet of snow in places."

Numerous patches of residual snow still decorating all areas of the campground was convincing evidence. Our arrival was on just the second day the campground had been open to the public that year. Predicting the water supply at the campground would be ready by the next day, Roy then took his leave as we finished clean-up after our lunch. We thanked him for the bounty of fresh water as he walked away with a wave.

With the temperature having risen into the fifties and real sunshine breaking through, Justin and I decided to walk around a bit, checking out the turf. We took a short hike along the main trail that leads to Mount McGuire for a mile or so, walking up another 270 feet of elevation. A beautiful lake was viewable below that did much to validate Roy's bragging of the area's scenic quality. I took a few photographs of the lake nestled within the mountain panorama, and then we walked back down to camp, feeling rather used up by the exercise. It was a modest practice run and did offset mild frustration with our lethargic energy levels.

Chargrilled pork chops with buttered corn and potatoes was our dinner, and then an early bedtime completed our second day in the mountains. The temperature plummeted once again as the night deepened, but thankfully fewer pee breaks were required, as our altitude acclimation neared completion. My nicotine and caffeine withdrawals were still present, though, as well as the freezing cold that once again forced total emersion within the sleeping bag. This time we broke out the long johns—thermal underwear—which did mildly improve the situation. To think that it was summertime… July 17th, in fact!

The Corps of Discovery set out north on September 1st with their Shoshone guide, who they called Old Toby.

"They were entering mountains far more difficult to pass than any American had ever attempted. The country is so remote and rugged that nearly two full centuries later it remains basically uninhabited. Clark described the route: *'Throe' thickets in which we were obliged to Cut a road, over rocky Sides where our horses were in [perpetual] danger of Slipping to Ther certain distruction & up & Down Steep hills… with the greatest dificuelty risque &c. we made 7.5 miles.'* On September 3rd, as the Expedition reached the Continental Divide and snow falling, Clark summed up the misery of the day, '*We passed over emence hils and Some of the worst roade that ever horses passed our horses frequently fell.*''' [12]

It got really bad before they made their way over the mountains. Old Toby himself got lost more than once, the snow and rugged landscape slowed the advance, near exhaustion of food supply occurred, and some of the horses ultimately were served up for dinner.

Justin and I would be entering the above-described terrain, going for broke in much the same way with our own expedition. We had prepared ourselves as well as could be known, given our own constraints of time, money, and a lack of mountain experience. People now did this kind of thing all the time here, so surely, we could do it, too. "*What one man can do, another man can do*"—to quote the dialogue spoken by Anthony Hopkins to Alec Baldwin in the movie *The Edge*.

We had lots of food. I had gone retro, to the diets popular at the beginning of the twentieth century. Unlike today, there were no abundance of diet programs for losing weight back then. Malnutrition was the much more common problem. Instead, a more appropriate advertisement proclaimed: "Let Us Make You Fat. It's no longer necessary to be thin, scrawny, and undeveloped." Our nine-day supply for six planned days would more than do the trick. Horses were not on the menu.

> More wisdom from Baden-Powell:
> "*A tenderfoot is sometimes inclined to be timid about handling an insensible man or a dead man, or even of seeing blood. Well, he won't be much use till he gets over such nonsense...*
> *In the case of hanging, cut down the body at once, taking care to support it with one arm while cutting the cord...*
> *And if he visits a butcher's slaughterhouse he will soon get accustomed to the sight of blood.*"

12 Ambrose

Day Nine…

Our third day in the mountains was once again near freezing with a heavy overcast sky and a strong breeze to greet the start of the day's activities. Justin dutifully assumed breakfast prep, and aside from suffering a grease fire in a pan of flame-fired bacon, he did well. No injury was suffered except to perhaps his confidence momentarily. The food was good enough to eat in its entirety, and that was success. We spent some time cleaning up, and then prepped our backpacks for the morrow. A couple of hours sitting and napping in the car allowed the dim solar rays to give relief from the cold morning mountain breezes that continued to swirl into the midday.

The first years of my involvement in sports proved conclusively that second-string reserve would be the best of my achievements. I was average height but underweight, near-sighted with poor corrective glasses, and not endowed with particularly good hand-eye coordination compared to my peers. Though an enthusiastic fan of baseball, football, and basketball, most of the time during games I participated by warming the bench. Practice makes perfect, and I developed perfection with running down the loose balls that I failed to throw correctly, catch, hit, or score with. I wasn't winning, even if the team was.

Justin was a marginally better athlete than I, and his stepdad, Ken, was available more than my own father had been to encourage and coach. Even so, Justin had lost interest in football and baseball by age twelve and had only continued to play because he thought I demanded it. Once learning that he preferred the bench to actually playing, I was heartbroken. I let him know that he should just play the games he liked, and expressed my regrets for any discomfort this confusion may have caused him. Ken's specialties were soccer, track, and field sports. Justin liked and excelled at those games.

Unfortunately, bullying is quite common for boys of average size or less at this age, and my suspicions were great that he might also be subject to that harassment, just as I had been. A couple of signals indicating possible bullying victimization are when a child noticeably becomes erratic with behavior, and academic performance suddenly declines. Justin had done well enough academically in school until about age twelve when some notable discipline issues occurred and his grades fell.

Uncertain as to what should be done, I consulted Randall, my old and enduring friend. With two children of the same age as my son, Randall recommended enrolling Justin in a martial arts school, where his own three children had done very well. They had all earned black belt rank at the Korean Tae Kwon Do Academy, at what proved to be a very modest tuition. They all were getting good grades, were models of good manners and generosity, and had befriended Justin when he had been a toddler.

After meeting with the instructor, James R., and checking out the academy, Debby, Ken, and I decided to give it a try. Since this experiment was my idea, I promised to finance and be responsible for delivering Justin to two of the classes per week, while Debbie or her husband would take him to a third night's lesson. This launched my son's Tae Kwon Do program where he also earned a black belt in the following three years.

Justin's enthusiasm for the sport was very pleasing. His instructor made the lessons fun and doted on the younger students with many special attentions. James R. also demanded the students get good grades in their regular schooling, requiring them to submit their report cards every semester. If they did not have at least a B-average, the kids would have to bring and do their homework at his classes instead of participating in the martial arts. Academia came first, and then the right was earned to have the fun.

It was a major relief to learn from one of his regular school friends, Jimmy W., that Justin wasn't being bullied anymore within six months of starting the program. Martial arts training does carry a sizable mystique. Jimmy was also a martial arts student at the academy and had made certain that word had gotten out of my son's new toughness. Justin's grades had rebounded and were his best ever. And from what was shared with me by his mother, Justin's behavior performance had also become exemplary. His participation in this Tae Kwon Do training succeeded in matching the desires of everybody concerned.

Additional training and performance in the Intra-Academy Forms and Sparring tournaments earned him rights to compete in the National KTA Tournament. The martial arts had paid great dividends. Participating in this tournament seemed a just reward for all of Justin's dedication, perseverance, and demonstrated success at all levels. His mother easily agreed to let him attend the tournament in Los Angeles, and I was very excited to chaperone and finance. Out to California Justin and I flew, as we accompanied the other qualifying students, several parents, and the instructor from the academy.

Justin was one of the older kids by then, a soon-to-be sophomore in high school. While on this excursion, he preferred the company of two other boys and a girl, all close to his age of fifteen. We attending parents kidded them about being Dorothy, the Lion, the Tin Man, and the Scarecrow as they were inseparable. But during the events, they cheered each other on as well as the younger "Munchkin" team members. All performed admirably in their own highly competitive events, but it was from the "Munchkins" that national gold medals were won for the academy—four in total. It was quite the spectacle. No one was injured, while self-confidence, camaraderie, and a well-deserved pride was shared by students, the instructor, and the parents perhaps most of all. Once and for all, James R. had provided me solid proof that Justin was a well-trained, tough hombre. Justin had competed with the best in the nation, and performed well as participant, team member, and a support to his classmates, admirably. A proud father I was.

In late afternoon, the winds finally died down and the sky cleared, with the temperature becoming much more tolerable. Justin and I decided to check out the lake we had seen on our previous day hike and try some fishing. We gathered the fishing gear and proceeded down a second trail toward that picturesque natural body of water named Golden Trout Lake, with hopes of also photographing some wildlife. The trail was short, and appeared wide and well-marked, so we dispensed with bringing a topographical map I had packed for the trip. It would get used enough the next day, on the real hike.

Somehow, even though the trail length was only two miles, we lost it before getting as far as half of the first mile. We began guesstimating, blazing our own trail farther down, intent on intersecting the true pathway. The angle of descent soon began to increase with no further sign of the trail, and then familiar altitude fatigue also began to set in. Definitely lost within fifteen minutes, we were thrashing about in an endless forest where the downward slope was rapidly increasing to precarious steepness. This became

Golden Trout Lake

most worrisome. I had no desire to become a "lost in the woods" statistic within a half-mile of the trailhead campground. The experience was more than a little unnerving. Reluctantly, we decided to scotch the fishing and photos idea and opted for getting back to the trailhead camp. The only direction of certainty was uphill. Reversing ourselves, we then trudged back the way we had come and did finally rejoin the lost pathway. We were panting heavily in the few minutes it took. Continuing until reaching the camp, our physical state was of being unexpectedly very tired, sweating, and thirsty. The walkabout had taken less than an hour and drinking water for this little excursion had also been forgotten.

Word of the campground tap water supply being potable and drinkable was delivered by Roy after our return, and he shared a bit more about the features of the trails to Mount McGuire we could plan to use. There were two different trails to the camping area near our wilderness destination. The shortest trail was measured at eight miles, while the second trail measured eleven miles.

One feature of the most direct and shorter trail was called the Beaver Slide. It was an alternative means of negotiating a steep descent from the top of a high ridge into an amphitheater bowl-shaped area on the mountainside. Known as a cirque, that geological feature offered opportunity for a bit of extra fun. At about the six-mile marker, the trail, after a gain of eight hundred altitude from our current campground, would arrive at the top of a high ridge. Normally the descent down the steep-sided ridge was via a switchback path. That trail would zigzag back and forth some 250 feet down, such that the rate of decline was not too precarious for packhorse traffic. But since the cirque was normally snow covered until mid-August, hikers could take a giant snow slide shortcut to the bottom. The idea did sound intriguing, and we were now very sympathetic to the idea of a shorter hike.

As evening drew near later, Justin and I rekindled the fire for some supper. With the wind having died down and the temperature warmer, hordes of mosquitoes once again chased us into our tent where we could eat dinner without inhaling a bug with every bite. Both of us found it amazing at the profligate numbers that attacked in cloud formation around the face. The only relief from them outside of shelter without a steady, helping breeze, was standing in the smoke of the fire, which gets old very quickly. One redeeming characteristic of these mountain mosquitos was that their bites didn't itch as much as the lower-altitude blood suckers do. We stayed inside playing cards until dark. Justin allowed me to win.

Sleep came sooner and was less interrupted this third night, and I reflected on our progress optimistically. My son had passed the fire-building test, as well as the first levels of cooking and tent camping. The actual hiking would be next, along with map reading and the final backpacking preparation. He was ready enough for the challenges, eager to perform and be tested, and chomping at the bit, I suspected. My own confidence was still strong, but I was clear that due caution would be a serious imperative. We would do this thing!

***

The solution to my childhood Scouting malaise ended on a Saturday afternoon of the following September after my Troop had folded. Mother had suddenly called me to the front door of our house and pointed to a boy walking along the sidewalk across the street.

"Go get that boy and tell him I want to talk to him," she commanded.

"What for?" I asked. "I don't know him, do you?"

"No," she said with impatience, "but he's a Boy Scout and I want to talk to him. Go get him and bring him back here to talk with me!"

Away I ran in pursuit of the fellow, who was clearly a Scout due to his uniform attire. His walk was deliberate with a real spring in his step. When I called out to him, "Hey, kid, stop!" he may not have heard me, or was ignoring this call out of the blue from a stranger. He did seem to increase his walking speed. Upon covering the interval that separated us, up close I said, "Hey, Boy Scout, stop! My mom wants you to come back to our house to talk to you."

My abrupt approach and loud communication seemed to momentarily startle him by the look on his face as he turned toward me. He was shorter than I and appeared younger. Once facing me directly, his expression changed quickly to a mix of quizzical interest and a friendly, if not amused, grin. He could also see my mother demonstrably waving from afar on our doorstep, and she shouted, "Come back over here!"

As I viewed the kid fully, it was immediately apparent why my mother had been so interested in this guy. He was dressed in what would constitute the sharpest parade Scout uniform I'd ever seen. It literally seemed to dazzle in the midday sun. As we approached the house, I introduced myself, and he likewise reciprocated, "Hi. My name is Hans P."

After being complimented by Mom on his sharp uniform, Hans enthusiastically explained that he usually didn't dress this way—rarely, in fact. He was returning from the Central Indiana Boy Scout Council's "Board of Review for Eagle Scout," which he had passed successfully after fulfilling all other requirements. It was a special occasion when he wore his Merit Badge sash, which contained twenty-one merit badges of accomplishment in seven neatly sewn rows. He further informed us that his dad was the Scoutmaster of his Troop, and that their weekly meeting place was just four blocks away. Their family lived in a house only two blocks down from ours, on the very same street. The reason we had never met was that he and his younger brother attended a different school and church. Hans agreed to relay Mom's request, "Have your dad call me when convenient about your Scout Troop." She gave him our telephone number on a slip of paper, and away he walked.

Surprisingly, Hans' dad called within about six minutes, barely enough time for the boy to have completed his walk home. Mr. P. offered to come right over! Since it was a leisurely Saturday, my parents agreed. He showed up at our front door in nearly a flash. With a big smile, this new Scoutmaster greeted Mom, Dad, my brother John (who was now the required age of eleven years old to be a Scout), and myself. There was a strange twinkle in the man's eye and an authentic warmth when he shook my hand, as if I might be special. His name was George P.

At our introductory meeting, he talked at length about several of the activities that the Scouts of his Troop engaged in: Scout meetings every week, a Scout camping event nearly every month, large multi-Troop District Camporees, regular skills-advancement demonstrations, five, ten, and even 20 mile hikes, the State Scout Fair event, canoe trips, a week of troop summer camping…Wow… Cool! This Troop also offered deep experience, with several other Eagle and Senior Scouts participating, of which Hans was the newest. He also disclosed that he himself was an Eagle Scout. Looking at me directly, Scoutmaster George P. said, "David, if you want to be an Eagle Scout, I promise you our program will have you become an Eagle."

George P. would ultimately prove to become one of the most influential adult leaders of my life. My brother and I both moved on to full-out Scouting, the way the program is designed to be taught and intended to be experienced. What I'd secured was a mentor for life, who lived the Scout Promise, Scout Law, Scout Motto, and Scout Slogan as a true exemplar of how it is done and how one should lead.

The first phrase of the Scout Oath describes who Mr. George P. was always being: *"On my honor, I will do my best to do my duty…"*

CHAPTER
SIX

Day Ten...

We arose early the next morning with excitement and intentionality. Breakfast of hot oatmeal, hard-boiled eggs, and fried Spam were consumed with orange juice, milk, and bananas to energize our start. My cravings for caffeine and nicotine had subsided to become tolerable, so we attended to all the basic camp chores with a bit more alacrity and competency. The tent was emptied and all non-packed items for the hike were moved to the car. The tent was collapsed, folded, and then attached to the frame of the backpacked gear we would be hauling to our next campsite. Food, water, extra clothing, and sleeping bags were all arranged for carry. The topographical maps were carefully included! Sunscreen was applied, insect repellent was administered, and we were ready. Saddling up our gear, we departed for the trailhead by ten thirty. With more than ten hours of daylight to cover the supposed eight miles to our next camp, the hike would place us close enough to photograph our mountain.

A morning sun was out and bright for the first time, and optimism was running high. Passing by a dozen college-age kids packing their own gear at the trailhead parking lot, observing them deal with a chaos of gear spread out and covering half of the entire area, we felt new confidence about ourselves and our own meticulous preparations. Day number four in the mountains had a reasonable start. We felt acclimated to the altitude, and that fed optimism. Unfortunately, these feelings proved to be short lived and too good to be true, especially for me.

A hiking trail book by Margaret Fuller describes the trail we were taking as follows: "From the Crags campground trailhead of 8,450 feet, one enters the wilderness. After zigzagging up a ridge of lodgepole pine trees, the trail contours above Golden Trout Lake to an 8,720-foot summit at a distance of one mile."

Within the first zig, I called out to Justin, "This isn't going to work because my pack is way too heavy. I'm not going to make it." This was my surrender statement, as the straps of the pack bit into my shoulders with teeth and felt like a crushing weight.

"No, Dad, you can make it; we're doing this," was Justin's committed, optimistic, and supportive response to me from a good fifty feet up ahead. "I can carry a little more in my pack," he added with full assurance. He returned to lend me a hand.

Justin redistributed about seven pounds of stuff from my pack to his, and we saddled up again to continue. The repack did seem to do the trick, because the bite of the straps and crush of the weight was reduced to just plain uncomfortable and heavy. I would deal with it. We reached the summit of the first hill after taking a couple of very short breaks to admire the lake we had seen two days before. The view was tremendous! We took yet another break there to rest and drink water, having worked up a sweat in the barely-fifty-degree weather.

The solar heat was dramatically warming when we were exposed directly, and the difference in temperature felt at least ten degrees cooler in the shaded areas of the trail. A fourth or fifth break in the first mile was a clear signal that my legs were tiring far sooner than I ever anticipated. It was my smoker's lungs that had been the expected weakness, particularly in the thinner air, but my legs were what pained the most. This was a surprise, since I often walked up to ten miles per day at my job, which involved carrying stuff weighing ten to thirty pounds all around the facility.

The trail continued on a declining slope for about four tenths of a mile, which was easier hiking, and on past a trail crossroad. The path then began ascending a second ridge on the main trail. This three-hundred-foot climb required me to stop several more times to rest the burning sensation in my calves and thighs. At the two-mile mark, we reached the first of several huge granite rock towers that exuded a spooky, almost forbidding presence when observed from their base. They reminded me of the giant alien worm creatures from the sci-fi movie *Dune*, jutting out of the ridge as much as seventy-five feet above us. There seemed to be a very odd, even fleetingly alien presence there. We were at an altitude of nine thousand feet, and a cool breeze sweeping through the tower-shaded area chilled the sweat from our exertions and motivated trekking on past some of the most interesting rocks of the hike. Over the next seven tenths of a mile, the trail descended from uneven ground along the ridgeline past a landmark known as Cathedral Rock.

Continuing the descent a couple more tenths of a mile, our hike reached another crossroads. One of these would be the trail to our mountain. The nine-thousand-foot altitude we'd climbed up to had been given back. It was here that Justin and I took a major thirty-minute break. We both now suffered very tired legs and stiff backs.[14] We consumed a lunch of Spam sandwiches, cheese, fruit, and water. The Spam was a new meat product for my son, and he did not particularly relish the flavor when served cold. But the extra fat content would be appreciated, if not the taste of it. Mustard helped! The food did wonders, as did the absence of the carried weight, and we began to revive a bit.

The group of college guys that we'd passed by at the trailhead hiked past us now, two or three of them stopping to take a short break and chat with us. They were a group of eleven on a two-week, school-sponsored biology research project for their master's degree program. The group was headed to a different lake area than we were. The hikers who stopped to chat a bit were perhaps also ready for a short break, but the rest filed on to the other trail. The fellows we spoke with mentioned they were studying some sort of salamander-type creature that was native to the area. Shortly, these students completed their own break with us and moved on, leaving us to our rest for a few more minutes. On reflection, these guys were in far better physical condition than I, looked better yet more lightly equipped, and had covered the distance in half of our time. Justin and I clearly shared the status of "Rookie."

Soon after we started out again, a young uniformed park ranger hiked past us from the trail we were following. Smiling acknowledgement, he reported all was clear up ahead and wished us a good time. This was a nice reassurance that at least, so far, we were on the correct trail and there were no barriers or obstructions to contend with. Onward we plodded.

The equipment Justin and I had pulled together for our trek had been acquired over the preceding year with utility, short experience, and frugality as primary constraints. We had gone out together several times to purchase our tent, hiking boots, illumination, sleeping bags, water canteens, and a host of other odds and ends, including fishing poles. Mistakes had been made by relying on some of the older, borrowed items like a dated military backpack and frame, foam ground pads, and a large, metal canteen. Further errors were the buying and/or packing of several items that were obsolete or would never be used, such as my recreational reading book, a huge camp light, and a four-month supply of extra batteries. Thus, our packs weighed far too much, perhaps exceeding a shared 100 pounds, when eighty pounds should have been the maximum. Our hands were also encumbered with odd items, like the fishing gear, that had not been attachable to our backpacks. The next stretch of trail would bring the overweight issue brutally home.

Three-and-a-half hours in, the map indicated that about half the distance had been covered on this shorter avenue we had chosen. The path would climb three hundred feet up a new wooded ridge to a third crossroad, and then continue another 680 feet up. The trail then would wander along the side of Fishfin Ridge at the summit. The increased rate of elevation in this section of the trail did not look particularly steep for the distance covered, but it was unrelenting and uninterrupted.

The burn in my legs and back returned within fifteen minutes, and I found myself forced to stop repeatedly as Justin trudged on ahead. We finally switched positions to stay in range of each other for quick mutual assistance. By the time half the distance up was traversed, I was taking steps no larger than from boot heel to toe and counting only fifty at a time between breaks. Un-f#@&-ing-believable! My body was breaking down to painful mush, like the wimps I had always hypocritically derided.

Though not particularly athletic, I considered myself in very good physical condition at forty-four years of age and 165 pounds. Just over one year prior, I had sprint-raced my already taller, longer-legged, high-school-track-team-member son in the four-hundred-meter dash wearing only penny loafers, and he using track running shoes. Yes, he had eclipsed me, but by just a three-meter margin. I had also done a full-out one-mile run in more steeply graded hilly terrain less than ten years before—in under eight minutes, without any training. That preceding spring, I'd regularly weight lifted at a gym, bench pressing two-hundred pounds, which was more than my own weight, and leg pressed 250 pounds in three sets of ten repetitions. These were no records of particular regard by any standard other than my own, but it wasn't sad and wimpy like this situation and my performance was degenerating into.

This bodily betrayal was as mentally hurtful as it was physical.

Dehydration alongside a deep exhaustion was beginning to have my mind play tricks. After continuing painfully for what must have been at least two hours, we finally reached the top of Fishfin Ridge. But again, the ground was uneven with substantial dips, and the wanderings required continued up-and-down-elevation walking…and the drinking water was now running very short.

Somewhere before the six-mile mark and the Beaver Slide, my body and mind began to break down altogether. The map no longer made sense to me, and I misread it badly. Confusing one of the lakes on the map for a substantial body of water visible through the trees, I became convinced that it was a mapped water feature, and though short of our objective, must suffice to be our destination. It appeared about 150 feet down and perhaps two hundred yards distant. The sky had darkened with overcast, and I had no doubt that the time must have been near six o'clock. Removing my pack, I did a quick reconnaissance ahead, which only revealed another switchback zigzagging up and over the top of a ridge in the opposite direction from the water below. Backtracking another one hundred yards or so revealed no trail downward to the water in that direction, either.

It was tantrum time lest I forget the seven magic words you shouldn't say on TV. Again, I only ranted for two minutes—maybe three? Once I'd spit out the demons within me to the all-hearing wilderness, a decision had to be made. We had to either stop there or continue and risk darkness overtaking us while still on a very narrow and precipitous trail. It was clear that we (or me, for sure) were on our last legs. The true distance to our planned destination was now unknown. Had we missed a turn and were not even located where I thought, or just short of where I reckoned? The Beaver Slide in the dark would be an impossible folly and still required nearly two more miles of additional hiking beyond it to the planned campground site.

Grasping for the "bird-in-hand," we blazed our own trail with some of the equipment downward to the water. The degree of descent was quite steep, exceeding a fifty-five-degree slope. The surface was mixed dirt, gravel, wild vines, moss, and grasses, forming a modest terracing. There were lots of small and larger trees to use for grabbing and slowing one's slide, so aside from the scare of nearly impaling myself on a protruding dead tree limb halfway down, I made it to the flat open ground surrounding the water intact.

Justin, in like fashion, followed with a portion of his equipment. We could see a stone fire ring and wood debris that meant folks had camped there before. So be it. This was our spot. I asked my son if he could manage climbing the ridge up to the trail to retrieve both of our backpacks, while I selected firewood to build a fire. He agreed readily. After a short rest, off we both went to our assigned tasks for creating our first official wilderness campsite.

A fire was burning by the time Justin brought down the second pack that included the tent. Our shelter was sighted on a dry grass area close to a big snow drift, laid out, and then raised. We commenced cooking up some canned chicken and Lipton instant rice. A futile searching of my pack and Justin's for Advil or aspirin forced desperate and premature measures be taken. I had packed a bottle of wine to celebrate our successful hike to our mountain, but the pain in my back was biting to such a degree that early consumption for medicinal purpose became the mandate. As we watched the water for our food boil, I shared a small glass with my son (Bad Daddy? Nope! Children in Europe drink wine at age six.) I then savored about half of what remained of the bottle before we ate dinner. One last goody I revealed to Justin as we ate the most delicious dinner was a can of Coca-Cola I had covertly packed. With eyes as big as saucers and a smile from ear to ear, he chuckled throughout the dinner as we consumed the beverage slowly, cherishing every drop.

Darkness was upon us soon after finishing our clean-up and dousing the fire. My son and I then stretched out in the tent talking for a few minutes. Discussing the trials of the hike, I praised his performance and apologized for my own. We both spoke optimistically about continuing the next day. After removing our boots, I was astounded that the two pairs of socks worn were literally dripping with the sweat of the day. Aside from a few foot blisters and bruised pride, no other injuries had been suffered. The wine did its work and relaxed me through updating my journal. The sleep following total exhaustion overcame the wakeful moments very quickly.

Just over seventy-five miles north of where we were, Lewis and Clark had crossed this Northern Rocky Mountains area in mid-September on their way to the Pacific.

"The worst days occurred as they trekked westward through freshly fallen snow, as Clark describes: 'I have been wet and cold in every part as I ever was in my life… passing emince Dificuelt Knobs Stones much falling timber and emencely Steep.'" [13]

Wild game animals were very sparse to supplement the already thin rations available, such that even a coyote was served as entrée one night.

"The captains ordered a colt from the horses killed and butchered, 'which we all Suped hartily and thought it fine meat.' The next day, their starving horses having wandered off in the night had to be recovered, which slowed departure until afternoon, and after only ten miles distance traveled, camp was made at a 'Sinque hole full of water.' The hunters had failed to secure sufficient wild game once again, so this 'compelled [them] to kill Something: a coalt being the most useless part of our Stock he fell a Prey to our appetites.'" [14]

The captains could see that their men's morale was very low and they were reaching the limits of their physical endurance. Their food supply was all but gone and finding game animals appeared hopeless. Lewis realized that the men, he himself, and Clark, were near the breaking point. But retreat was not an option, for *"they would rather die than quit".* [15]

They had to go on, and did, by eating more filet of packhorse until sighting the end of their mountain crossing two days later. Completing a 160-mile forced march though these mountains in eleven days, the explorers were welcomed by the Nez Perce Indian tribe with shelter, food, and new wherewithal to complete their passage to the mouth of the Columbia River and the Pacific Ocean. These Nez Perce Indians of Idaho would remain one of the white man's strongest and most peaceful allies in the West for the next seventy years.

Day Eleven...

Wilderness Camp

The so-called lake we had camped beside was all but completely frozen over at dawn and was actually a snow-melt pond with no fish or other visible aquatic life. The exertions of the hike had been brutal, and with the morning we both had stiff, sore muscles and were severely debilitated by lingering fatigue. There would be little movement that day. It was agreed our condition was still prohibitively too worn-out, and our fresh water supply was exhausted. A chest-high snowdrift was close by the tent, so we went about the minimal task of gathering wood for a fire to boil the snow down to water most of the day. Rehydrating ourselves was the main critical task, as well as resupplying our camp cooking and cleaning needs and replenishing our canteens for the morrow. Two other tasks of note were performed, and wilderness camping required at least one of them.

Aside from the basic human needs for air, water, and food, just like the law of gravity (what goes up must come down), what goes in must come out. Exhale, urinate, and...the particularly important necessity of voiding the bowels...bowel movement, taking a dump, pinching a loaf, taking a sit, taking a moment, taking a rest, etc....an extensive list of terms designed to cut short the discussion about something most folks must deal with every day. Nice and gentle terms, or coarse and even vulgar, only proctologists are very comfortable with discussion of the topic with any intimate detail. Many city folks, civilized by indoor plumbing, may never go primitive camping because of being confronted by this subject. For women, the urination issue is often also considered a big problem. But deal with it I did, and was a better man for it.

The first step was to dig a ten-inch-deep cat-hole latrine for this necessary bodily function, of which I put to good use. The rules of wilderness activities made strong request that all sign of human presence be as inconspicuous and eco-friendly as possible, and some folks even bag their waste and hike out with it. Justin refused any relief by either of those primitive-sounding methods, civilized to a far more genteel accommodation when engaged in that biological routine. My warning that it would be better dealing with crapping there instead of the next day on the trail inspired no compromise to his view on the matter. He said that he'd rather take his chances by holding off until safely back to town. The two-extra mosquito bites I endured while thus engaged discounted my argument, but not my relief. We did have plenty of hand sanitizer and tissue.

The second task I felt important was to demonstrate the firearm. I could see from Justin's distracted, muted conversation and wary behavior that it might calm his unspoken safety concerns about the possibility of encountering an aggressive predator. Calling him over, he stood just behind my shoulder with earplugs to view a single firing. We had made camp in another cirque formation of the ridge, a small amphitheater-shaped area looking out over endless tracts of the wilderness. The discharge of the pistol was as loud as ever, amplified by the natural acoustics. My aim being just a bit high, I missed a piece of floating wood debris some twenty-five feet out in the water of the melt pond. A three-foot-high geyser of water erupted where the slug impacted the tranquil surface just behind the target, adding further visual impact to the sound and bright, one meter flame spouting from the pistol.

As I turned to ask what he thought, his relieved smile signaled his concerns had vanished.

"Good enough," he replied, and a new confidence in his movements about camp jump-started both of our energy levels for the next couple of hours. I later found that the discharge of any firearms during summer months was prohibited, but I might have risked the exercise anyway, just for the peace of mind it bestowed.

A more hike-able avenue back up to the trail was located while collecting some firewood, and I took some photos of massive rock towers that were part of this cirque formation, as well as our tent pitched serenely next to the melt pond. Prepping foods for lunch and dinner were my tasks while Justin gathered more wood. The day was overcast and chilly but stayed fortuitously dry without too much breeze. We settled in, resting, napping, and maintaining the fire into the early evening.

My son was evidently fairly tight-lipped about any girlfriends with his mother, and Debby was "dying to know. Make him tell you on your trip." These had been her instructions. "He won't tell me anything," was a major complaint of hers.

Broaching this more sensitive topic was attempted during our slow time. I asked, "Do you have any affections for any of the girls in your life?" I had not noticed any directly and was somewhat curious myself.

"No, there is nobody special," he responded.

"What about the girl from the martial arts academy that you took to the dance last winter?" I pressed.

The girl I inquired about was my son's age, a really beautiful and polite young lady, who also held a Tae Kwan Do black belt. It was at least plausible that they might be a couple, in secret, and a handsome couple at that.

"Angela and I just went out that one time. She didn't seem to have much fun at the dance," he elaborated. "Being from a different high school, she didn't know anyone else there and had no one to talk to. And, she is very shy, you know. The icy, cold, and miserable weather that night didn't help."

"So, you haven't asked her out since? Was she mad or pissed at you?"

"Evidently, she wasn't too impressed, I guess," Justin explained. "I've only seen her once since then at the academy, and she just said, 'Hi!' and left before I could talk to her again. She's gone her own way, I think."

"So, there isn't anyone else you're a bit more than friends with at the high school," I furthered the interrogation.

"Nope! I'm just friends with the other girls I know. Nothing special."

"Well, your mom is going to be very disappointed, Son. Sorry!

She put me up to this. Just trying to keep her happy with some gossip about her son, ya know. You have plenty of time, Justin. Trust me on that."

Taking inventory of our adventure and the situation we were confronting, the next day's plan of action was obvious. My son had insisted he needed to return home within the next six days to begin his soccer team practices. Deeper penetration into the wilderness to seek our mountain would jeopardize that agenda. The fact that our bodies were beaten and worn out from just one day of backpacking, with the blisters, bug bites, sunburn, and prolonged cold nights having taken their toll, it was difficult to imagine continuing. Being semi-lost with no clear idea of how much farther we needed to hike, and realizing that every step further would mean retracing those same steps in addition to the ground already hiked, we were now quite intimidated. We agreed continuing farther toward the mountain was probably ill-advised. With such time constraints, returning to town needed to be our next move.

Aside from a few momentarily interesting birds, we had viewed no other wildlife except a squirrel. Though the forested mountains and great rocks had an awesome and breathtaking beauty, the ground was unforgiving and hostile to the inexperienced and unprepared stranger. A vague sense of being an unwanted intruder in this corner of the world could at times be felt and was amplified by the near-empty landscape. The weather had been mostly overcast, almost gloomy, the winds blustery, and the temperatures required all the extra layers of clothing we had packed. We had plunged into the wilderness with a goal of photographing Mount McGuire, our namesake mountain, and it seemed we had failed… by just a day? Feelings of incompletion, coming up short, and disappointment were a background presence as we made provision for the hike back to the trailhead, scheduled to start at first daylight on the morrow.

Our campfire dinner of chicken and rice was again simple fare, but more than adequate. The last half bottle of wine and a second Coca-Cola proved to be delicious and relaxing. The ministering to our sore blisters showed improvements. A game of chess, a couple of card games, and then a less-interrupted sleep came early and easily.

In 1884, Frederick Burnham married his childhood sweetheart, Blanche, and they returned to California to settle down and tend an orange grove. He transitioned from frontiersman to Freemason and was to stay active in that organization all his life. But soon enough, the more vibrant activities of prospecting and scouting drew him away from the settled-down pursuits. The government had announced the official closing of the American Frontier in 1890. Upon hearing stories of a new frontier in South Africa, Frederick sold what little he owned and set sail with his wife and baby to Durban, South Africa in 1893. His plan was to work as a scout for a railroad there, which was being constructed by the famous industrialist Cecil Rhodes.

While trekking one thousand miles north to Matabeleland in an American buckboard wagon pulled by six American mustangs with his wife and son, a war broke out between the white pioneers of the British South African Company and the black Ndebele tribal chief, King Lobengula. This was the First Matabele War, and Burnham signed on as a scout with the Company upon arrival. He was sent ahead with a small group to report the situation back to an advancing British column intent on ending the war quickly by a surprise capturing of the rebel king.

A patrol under a Major Allan Wilson, with Burnham as chief scout, located but failed to trap King Lobengula, who had fled ahead of the British main advance. Their small unit was surrounded and heavily outnumbered. Burnham, with two other men, was ordered to break through the enemy ring and bring up reinforcement. They successfully escaped, but the remaining men were overwhelmed after running out of ammunition and all killed to the last man. Called the Shangani Patrol and Wilson's Last Stand, it is the South African equivalent to the American Alamo and Custer defeats, glorified every year during White History Month.

King Lobengula contracted smallpox and died the following month, and the Ndebeli tribesmen made peace very soon after as they were now leaderless and had suffered horrific casualties from the British firepower provided by the newly developed technology of death called the Maxim automatic machine gun. In May of the following year, the British proclaimed the homeland of the Ndebeli the British territory (and future nation-state) of Rhodesia in honor of the guiding hand of progress provided by the industrial companies of Cecil Rhodes.

Frederick Burnham next oversaw and led the Northern Territories British South African Exploration Company expedition that established the existence of rich copper deposits in Rhodesia. Rewarded for that expedition, he became an elected Fellow of the Royal Geographical Society.

Day Twelve...

Highly motivated for our return to civilization on day six of the mountain wilderness, we were! Seven nights of sleeping on hard ground, five nights of contending with the mosquito hordes, and the penetrating cold nights reminiscent of winters back home had taken a toll.

We had eaten, packed, and were carefully ascending out of the cirque, up the steep side of the ridge to the trail above, by 6:40 A.M. Judging that it would take as long to return as it had to get there, I estimated a seven-hour hike back to the car. Fresh legs and slightly lighter packs allowed us to enjoy more of the fantastic mountaintop views from the trail, and the mostly downhill slope required fewer rest breaks for my legs. We retraced our visible footsteps in the dust of the trail, and realized no other folks had traversed this way during our time on the ridge. It lent credence to the experience of being perched on the edge of civilization and humanity as we gazed over the panorama of forested mountains stretching out over what appeared to be hundreds of miles, as far as the eye could see. The sun was shining full force in about two hours, and our moods improved when the solar rays renewed our energies and added a bit more kick to each step.

From the top of Fishfin Ridge, a photo shot of what we suspected might be Mount McGuire finished the roll of film in the camera. I became stymied by the film reloading process, however. The camera was very new to me and much more complicated than any I'd ever previously owned. Regardless, it was certain there were many good photographs captured of our adventure, so my disappointment was small. My next thoughts hoped that the vehicle would start without major difficulty. Multiple prayers were mumbled as we hiked, asking that we would make the trailhead at a decent hour and return to town that very evening. Mental promises were fervently made of clean living for the future and sacrifices to God. We arrived back at the trailhead parking area within the estimated time, at about 2:30 P.M. We signed ourselves out at the hiker's stand for Roy, such that no false rescue of us would commence, and then hurriedly repacked the vehicle. I then said another prayer for the car's health while strapping in, just before turning the ignition key.

Va-va-va-Roooom, on the second try the engine roared. We were blasting off and speeding down the mountain at an awesome three to five miles per hour. The first twelve miles were still absolutely, the most viciously rutted and rocky thing, and I still have difficulty referring to that thing as a "road." As we crept along, speed increased modestly in the same fashion on our return to Salmon as it had decreased on the way up the mountains. On the ride down, there was plenty of time to recount our experiences between prayers that the vehicle held together...what was and wasn't great, things to fix, replace, or acquire, and what to do differently—like actually climb that mountain next year, if in fact we had found it after all.

The sun was still well up when we arrived in town, the air a summery July-esque seventy-seven degrees. A motel option was chosen rather than returning to the local campgrounds for another night under canvas. An establishment named Motel Deluxe accepted our supplications for a room and we then fully returned to twentieth-century conveniences of habitation. From extremes of survival itself to the lap of luxury, we experienced once again hot showers, a flushing toilet, and beds with mattresses, clean sheets, and pillows! Unapologetically, I lounged about with a fine tobacco cigarette, my first purchase upon reaching the edge of town.

The Salmon River Coffee Shop was open and once again offered wide dinner menu choices, as well as a cocktail from the adjoining bar next door that our waitress obligingly provided. Appreciation of the relatively simple things in our modern world became a bright distinction that my son and I marveled at that night. After dinner, we walked along the small town's main street to the movie house and watched the action-thriller movie *The Rock* while eating popcorn for dessert. The final pleasure of the day was sleeping in our individual, warm double beds, stretching widely and relaxing, with no wake-up call to disturb sleeping late into the next morning.

CHAPTER
SEVEN

Day Thirteen...

The town of Salmon, Idaho, was settled in the 1860s and reported a population of 186 people by 1870. The architecture of the main-street buildings of Salmon still exude the spirit of a western frontier community, with several high-fronted nineteenth-century styled mercantile shops and the historic two-storied, red brick Grand Hotel, now converted to a restaurant-bar. The last census reported a stable population of just over 3,100 people. Salmon is the largest town in the east-central region of the state, averages about ten inches of rain per year, and reports an average yearly high temperature of 58.3 degrees Fahrenheit with an average yearly low of 30.8 degrees. It is at 3,944 feet above sea level, and mountains are in close view in every direction.

Ranching, mining, and timber harvesting were the primary economic activities of the area initially, but the local economy now revolves around the recreational industry, such as river rafting, camping, fishing, and wild game hunting. There are quite a number of restaurants, bars, lodging facilities, back-country transportation services, and small shops in town to accommodate the locals and visitor traffic, plus national, state, and county infrastructures like schools, fire, water, power utilities, and the regional headquarters for the U.S. Forest Service and Bureau of Land Management. The racial profile is over ninety-seven percent white, and the religious profile is predominantly of several Christian denominations.

While having our breakfast at the coffee shop, Justin and I decided to stay an extra night for more extended recuperation, to locate and use a laundromat, find a photographer to help switch the camera film, and check out what other jewels may be available in town. We soon found a photography shop where the kind owner politely showed ignorant me where the film compartment latch was located on my camera. A laundromat was also found that provided drop-off cleaning service, and we soon were once again able to wear fresh clothing, which after seven dirt-covered days felt quite special.

Completing our tasks, we walked about the central four-block business district, investigating the variety of interesting shops. We discovered the small Lemhi County museum, where validation of our days in the mountains became visually clear upon study of an accurately formed model of the area's topography, including the wilderness section we'd just returned from. We could clearly see that our mission of securing a photo of our mountain had been a success, and the fine detail of the model implied that a climb might be accomplished without the ridiculous dangers of a Matterhorn or Everest. This was a possibility we both contemplated for the remaining days of the vacation.

Our motel room included a kitchenette, so we visited the grocery and purchased dinner to eat-in, and some road food for our departure the next day. Justin had an interesting interaction at the store when one of the young kids working there gave him a wave to acknowledge him, and struck up a friendly conversation. The boys were about the same age, and this townsman had recognized us from the previous week. He had decided to say, "Howdy," and check out what Justin was about. The friendliness impressed my son, as it was not so common back home. His impressions of the town turned much more favorable, matching my own after this little episode. *A Scout is friendly.*

I never fail to find it interesting that such an effortless personal acknowledgement can make such positive impact, and seems so uncommon an experience. One thing our stay in the wilderness provoked was a renewed appreciation of humanity and in the common interaction with people again.

The Lewis and Clark Expedition stayed with the Nez Perce Indian tribe for fourteen nights to recover from passage of the central spine of the Northern Rockies.

"Lewis tried to describe his emotions: 'the pleasure I now felt in having triumphed over the rocky Mountains and descending once again to a level and fertile country where there was every rational hope of finding a comfortable subsistence for myself and party can be more readily conceived than expressed, nor was the flattering prospect of the final success of the expedition less pleasing.'

His journal continues describing the *'extremely trying conditions'; 'We suffered everything Cold, Hunger & Fatigue could impart.'"* [16]

Though the sustenance gathered during this layover was wanting, and nearly all the party suffered bouts of stomach illness and dysentery, the men now set about to build canoes for a resumption of water passage to the Pacific. On October 6th, 1805, they set out down the Coldwater River, which would merge with the Snake River, then join with the Columbia River and continue to the Pacific Ocean. Arriving near the coast in mid-November, "Clark records, *'Ocean in view! O! the joy.'"* [17]

Clark had also recorded his distance calculation that the expedition had traversed to the Pacific. *"Ocian 4142 Miles from Mouth of Missouri R."* [18]

The explorers built a modest stockade shelter in early December, just south of Young's Bay, naming the outpost Fort Clatsop. The Corps of Discovery wintered there peacefully among the Chinook and Clatsop Indian tribes of that region until the spring of 1806. This American occupation in Oregon would serve as the second foundational cornerstone to the claim by the United Sates of the area, the first claim based on a previously established trade outpost seventeen years prior by American Naval Captain John Kendrick on Vancouver Island. Though the Russians, Spanish, and British all had their own historic claims based on fur-trading outposts, it would be the far more dynamic, rapid, and permanent American pioneer settlements established there during the next fifty years that would guarantee sovereignty over the territory.

"On March 23rd, Lewis records bidding a final adieu to Fort Clatsop as the Americans began their return to the east via the Columbia River. The explorers were now traveling light, having consumed, depleted, or traded away the vast majority of trade goods, equipment, and accouterment." [19]

The journey upriver was strenuous work, but the villages of the Nez Perce were reached by May 4th. There the Americans bivouacked until June 10th, awaiting the snow to melt in the Rockies enough to continue their journey home. The Nez Perce then guided the Corps of Discovery back over the Bitterroot Range of the Rockies into Montana near the city of Missoula, where the captains split into two groups. The larger group was to retrace

16-19 Ambrose

their return down the Missouri River, as led by Lewis. Clark was to move a smaller exploration party over to the headwaters of the Yellowstone River and follow it down to where it joined the Missouri. They would rejoin Lewis there.

Day Fourteen...

Excellent preparations during our last evening in Salmon ensured a very early departure on day fourteen. By seven o'clock that morning, we were packed, loaded, checked out of the Motel Deluxe, and fueling the vehicle. The HondaCar had been, once again, hesitant to restart after receiving gas, requiring four ignition attempts. With it again running rough and balky at first, my worries about our vehicle would continue. Once up to speed and heading north, the engine smoothed itself out as we retraced our way along the Salmon River and back up the mountain to the Lost Trail Pass at the Continental Divide.

On our descent back into Montana, we passed the Big Hole National Battlefield, a semi-famous site where one of the last of large "conflict resolutions" between the U.S. Government and the American Indian tribes west of the Mississippi River took place. It was the turn of the Nez Perce to rebel in 1877.

We decided to bypass visits to Yellowstone Park, the Big Hole Battlefield of the Nez Perce, and the Little Bighorn National Battlefield due to my car worries. Compensating small excitement was visually beheld later by observing a large wildfire burning several hundred acres of grassy rangeland on the Crow Indian Reservation near the Interstate just before we crossed back into Wyoming. Firefighter trucks at the roadside, two helicopters circling about, and flashing lights of highway patrol cars directing the slowing traffic provided some scenic drama. Proceeding on until the sun was setting, about 650 miles were covered back to Devils Tower. With darkness coming on fast, it was a timely place to camp for the night. After paying the camping fee by check, my register balance was reduced to an interesting $666. The campground was well appointed and our practiced set-up routine went smoothly, as did a dinner of chargrilled burgers. The sleep was restful, so evidently the native or primordial spirits there did not object to our presence.

Devil's Tower and surrounding Monument Park

Indian tribes including the Arapaho, Crow, Cheyenne, Kiowa, Lakota, and Shoshone had, and still have, cultural and geographical ties to the Devils Tower monolith. These and other Native American groups hold the area as sacred. Their various names for the monument included Aloft on a Rock, Bear's House, Bear's Lodge, Home of Bears, Bear's Tipi, and Grizzly Bear Lodge. The renaming of the tower by white men was due to a translation error that occurred when the interpreter of Colonel Richard Dodge mistranslated it as named Bad God's Tower, which morphed into Devil's Tower.

According to the Kiowa and Lakota tribes, some girls were playing when several giant bears began chasing them. To escape, the girls climbed atop a rock and prayed to the Great Spirit to save them. The Great Spirit made the rock rise from the ground toward the heavens so that the bears could not reach them. The bears tried to climb the rock and left deep claw marks on the sides, visible on the tower to this day. The bears failed however, slipping back down because it was too steep. When the girls rose to the sky, they were turned into the star constellation the Pleiades. The other Indian tribes have similar stories.

As interpreted by Ancient Alien theorists, the monolith could be a space port for inter-planetary or inter-galactic vehicles. Another of their theories is that Devils Tower is really a planetary defense installation that friendly aliens currently use or used in the past. It somehow will focus magnetic energy into a death ray that defends Earth from asteroids and other extraterrestrial alien races that are hostile to mankind. If UFOs arrived in the night, we slept through it, and the aliens were gone by sunrise the next day. Steven Spielberg's movie set, up close and personal, and only the spaceships and aliens were missing... or did the aliens leave evidence behind?

Day Fifteen...

Our takeoff on the morning of July 24th from Devils Tower was frustratingly slow, departure delayed by lethargy and my lack of previous urgency. By the time we had eaten, packed up the vehicle, and were ready for the road it was well past ten o'clock. The HondaCar started with difficulty and was running very roughly, unwilling to idle without continuous pedal control to maintain steady RPMs. I dared not turn off the ignition when stopping for gasoline and restroom breaks for the remainder of the day.

Justin was doing a lot of sleeping in the car as he had done the previous day, which irritated me by the afternoon. That he wasn't awake and finding the grand landscapes enjoyable and stimulating seemed such a waste. I barked at him more than once to try and stay awake, if for no other reason than to assist me in fighting my own drowsiness. He was clearly feeling of little help as the driving lessons had been a bust, and he probably felt the need to check out from the tension my personal worries were creating. He did comply as best as he could with some reluctant chit-chat, but then had to endure my every opinion of each subject he bravely volunteered for my scrutiny. He was a courageously tolerant soul during the return. We finally chugged into Sioux Falls, the engine sounding worse than ever, and my predetermination was to give Scott, the Honda mechanic man, a call first thing in the morning. As a precaution, I backed the vehicle into the parking space in case of trouble.

Baden-Powell and Fredrick Burnham met, soldiered, and worked together starting in 1896 during yet another Native African insurrection called the Second Matabele War. The Ndebele (Matabele) people had once again revolted against the authority of the British South Africa Company in the country known today as Zimbabwe, where it is celebrated there as The First Chirmurenga. It was during this war that Robert Baden-Powell was educated in American woodcraft by Frederick Burnham, as they became well acquainted when leading military intelligence scout patrols together into the Matobo Hills.

The Industrial Revolution witnessed a great social change as agrarian populations were shifting from the countryside to large towns and cities. Both men recognized that the changing nature of how wars were being fought required some method of preparing urbanized young men in traditional outdoor skills. They were no longer being taught the basic and fundamental skills of the past that had ensured survival. What loomed then was a matter of future national security.

B-P and Frederick held several long talks about a broad program of woodcraft for young men that was rich in exploration, fieldcraft, and self-reliance. This would form the core of Baden-Powell's outdoor program and Code of Honor for his *Scouting for Boys*. The two men stayed engaged in these discussions over the following years, continuing to nurture the Scouting movement into the worldwide youth organization it is today. There are currently 34 million participants in Scouting worldwide as of 2016.

Eagle Scout Hans P. showed up three evenings after our introduction and invitation, to escort my brother and I to our first meeting with this new Boy Scout troop. He also spent several minutes with us prior to our departure, coaching my brother John and I on what was required for the weekly uniform inspection and what scouting materials to bring. This Troop took formalities very seriously.

It turned out to be quite the show—in more ways than one. We arrived at the church a few minutes early to the hustle and bustle of setting up the room for thirty attendees. Warmly greeted by Mr. P., we were then introduced to several of the adult leaders, the older Senior Scouts, and Hans' younger brother, Fred. The Scouts themselves ranged in age from eleven to eighteen years old, and the achievement ranks included at least three Eagles. All were very friendly and sharply dressed in full uniform, which was quite different from my previous Troop (it had been rare that even a third of the Scouts had attended in even partial uniform). The kids in this Troop embraced inspection as an opportunity to display a bit of pomp, pageantry, and pride.

There was also a special event. It was the viewing of a movie filmed during their last Scout outing—a canoe trip on one of the local rivers. Though filming is common today, back in the 1960s, this was no small feat. The cameras of that day were bulky and complex, requiring no small amount of skill and practice. Given what occurred and was caught on film, it was quite a show of hilarity, with the fast running river waters winning many of the skill challenge episodes. This Troop did a lot of very cool stuff on the edge. I'd found my crowd. My "Road to Eagle Scout" was now nearly clear. It's said that only one out of a thousand scouts achieve the rank of Eagle, and I was determined to be one of that select group.

About eighteen months after I had joined Scoutmaster George P.'s Boy Scout Troop, I completed all skills and requirements to be awarded the rank of Eagle Scout. Mr. P. did keep his promise to me. All five of my brothers would also earn this distinction over the next twelve years. The results my father had observed with me compelled him to eventually serve as a Scoutmaster himself for my brothers, and achieve several adult leadership awards to boot. For a brief time, my brothers and I were tied with the national record of six Eagles Scouts in a single family. The Mayor of our city, on hearing of the news, requested we come to his office for a photograph to be taken with us. A pretty good outcome, seeded by my Dad's small, even a bit reluctant action of setting up an improvised tent for his young sons wanting to "camp out" in the back yard so many years ago.

Day Sixteen...

The Honda would not start the next morning, confirming my suspicions from the evening before. A call to the dealership produced a tow very quickly, though Scott was off duty that day. Tim, the mechanic who had worked on the car previously, began an inspection right in the dealership lot. Justin and I walked up the street to a bagel shop for coffee and some eats. The service was quick at the eatery, so we munched bagels, sipped coffee, and wondered what might be our next move if the car was finally done. After an hour, we meandered back up the street to the car dealership to face the music.

By the time we returned, Tim had a complete diagnosis, reporting that two of the four engine cylinders were not firing and we needed a new battery. The car had held together just over 2,100 miles, exceeding all expectation, and then pushed past the limit that we had speculated on when departing from this place just two weeks previously. The mechanic switched out the battery, cleaned the distributor cap, and then declared the Honda roadworthy, a delay of just over three hours having elapsed. *Cha-ching!* went the cashier, and with a mental sigh of relief, the HondaCar ignition fired up once again. We drove out of Sioux Falls at the noon hour, our chariot yet again passing mile markers at better than one per minute, homeward bound on our final leg. Two more incidents of memorable note occurred on this return passage.

We made few stops along the way, eating fast-food and minimizing bathroom breaks to the point of pain. But at one such stop in Iowa, patience was sorely tested. We arrived behind another group of travelers who were up to similar tasks, comprising some twelve people in two vehicles. The single working restroom required a wait that ended up being over twenty-five minutes long, and the ugliest thoughts for my fellow man and woman occurred in that nugget of time. We survived silently, but it was surely the most severe test of patience for the day.

Darkness fell as we entered our neighboring state of Illinois, and this time our truck stop choice was a good one. The food and service was most excellent, even if the fuel prices were higher than our average of the trip. The nearer to home we advanced, the livelier Justin's conversation grew as we considered if we would attempt another road trip to climb our mountain the next year. My own enthusiasm had grown as we debated the pros and cons, and what would be required of us to accomplish it. Justin's agreement with this new expeditionary project validated that perhaps I had not, in fact, been as bad a character with him as I had feared.

We arrived at my son's home at around two o'clock in the morning. A call to his mom some five minutes earlier allowed a smooth unloading and entry into the house, safe and sound. Justin was returning just in time for the first day of his soccer team practice, with hopes running high that he would play on the team that autumn. He had played the sport since childhood, and even helped with coaching the younger kids with Ken, but he had not played on a team himself for the past four years. Justin's four-year participation in martial arts had dominated his afterschool hours. He was now very eager to fulfill a long-held and delayed desire to play soccer again. After a final hug and farewell, I continued to my own house, which was about a twenty-minute drive through the night away.

"But beware of professional football," wrote Lord Baden-Powell, "*in itself... a grand game for developing a lad physically and also morally, for he learns to play with good temper and unselfishness, to play in his place and play the game, and these are the best of training for any game of life. But it is a vicious game when it draws crowds of lads away from playing the game themselves to be merely onlookers at a few paid performers. ...My heart sickens at ...thousands of boys and young men, pale, narrow-chested, hunched-up, miserable specimens... all of them learning to be hysterical as they groan or cheer in panic unison with their neighbors. The worst sound of all be the hysterical scream of laughter that greets any little trip or fall of a player... Get the lads away from this. Teach them to be manly, to play the game whatever it may be, and not be merely onlookers and loafers.*"

While fumbling with the key in the darkness, I saw my roommate peeking through the front door's venetian blinds.

"Hi, Jim! I'm back!" I called out as he slowly opened the door, noticeably stern.

"You just scared the shit outta me coming in at this hour," was his greeting. It was about 2:30 A.M., after all.

"Who else were you expecting at this time?" I responded innocently.

"For this neighborhood, it could be anybody. Crackheads, rapists, thieves, there's all kinds of bad people—you know that!" he reprimanded.

Glancing down at his arm, I noticed his .357 revolver slowly being lowered.

I really should have called ahead. *I should have written more than just a postcard*, I thought. Attempting a comic response, I said, "All right, Jim. Thanks for not shooting me. And the neighbors thank you, too. No time to be getting a reputation as a cantankerous old drama queen, now is it?" I chuckled nervously.

One last and final "close call" emphasized that it was a very lucky trip, indeed.

CHAPTER
EIGHT

Every vacation usually ends at the point where the participants arrive back from whence they started, and the retelling of the adventures go on for about two weeks. Then it becomes pretty much old news and fades away, perhaps briefly revisited every five or twenty years when conversation reminds or old boxes of photos are reopened during spring cleaning.

I feel that road trips are sometimes a bit different for a couple of reasons. Some often have greater long-term impacts due to the mission that the excursion is designed to accomplish. Another reason is that the aftermath of certain road trips might contain decisive encounters, actions, and/or commitments that overshadow the exploits experienced, more sharply focus them, or become a focus unto themselves.

The first father-son road trip in Western culture might be attributed to Marco Polo and his father, Niccolo, who set out from their home in Venice, Italy, on a mega adventure. Bound for the Far East, by the time they returned from China and the Orient they had traveled an estimated fifteen thousand miles to lands of myth, legend, mystery, and fable, over a period of twenty-four years. Though they didn't have an automobile, they did have a mission to accomplish.

Their goal was to fulfill a direct and specific command by none other than the most powerful man in the world of that era, Kublai Khan, Emperor of the Mongol Empire, the most powerful, culturally refined, and technologically advanced civilization at that time. The Polos' goal was to fulfill this mission while conducting trade, acquiring fabulous riches and treasures, and returning home to Venice with them.

Marco was yet another person who didn't have the most idyllic or traditional of childhoods with his father. In fact, he didn't even meet his dad until he was a teenager. Niccolo was a rather successful Venetian merchant who traded with the Near East. He and his brother, Maffeo, had moved to Constantinople, leaving Marco's pregnant mother behind with family in Venice. The brothers had set up a trade office there at the Byzantine capitol, with other outposts in the Crimea and the western part of the Mongol Empire. The brothers moved eastward over the following few years in pursuit of more lucrative trade. Eventually they reached the Court of Kublai Khan of the Yuan Dynasty at Dadu, present-day Beijing, China. Niccolo was accepted as an ambassador for the Catholic Pope in Rome.

The Emperor of Cathay commanded that Niccolo deliver a letter to Pope Clement IV, requesting that the Pope send one hundred educated people from Europe to China to teach his people Christianity and Western customs. He also requested some oil from the lamp of the Holy Sepulcher, the most revered place of worship in Christendom.

The oil was thought to have mystical qualities once blessed, and possible supernatural powers once subjected to the miracle of Holy Fire, as was witnessed by Eastern Orthodox pilgrims at the Holy Sepulcher every year. A blue light emanates within the tomb of Jesus Christ, said to be located there. The light gradually rises to form a column containing a form of fire, which also is said to spontaneously light the oil lamps and candles around the church.

Niccolo was presented with a paiza, a golden tablet that would obtain the holder food, lodging, and horses throughout the Mongol Empire, just like a Gold MasterCard today. It would also serve as authentication of Kublai Khan's communication to the Pope. The brothers departed China for the Kingdom of Jerusalem. The Ninth Crusade was still being fought in the Holy Land to regain and maintain Christian pilgrims' access, thus the blessed oil was obtained. Arriving there in 1269 or 1270, they learned of the Pope's death, and given the delays of politics in those days, returned to Venice to await election of a new Pope.

Niccolo was to finally meet with his son, Marco, who was by then fifteen or sixteen years of age. Marco had been raised in Venice by his mother and then his aunt and uncle after his mother's death. He had received a good education, learning the mercantile subjects including numbers, currencies, appraising, and the handling of cargo ships. But only then as a young adult did a relationship with his father begin.

In 1271, Niccolo, Maffeo, and Marco Polo departed Venice, Papal letters in hand from the new Pope (Gregory X) for the

Chinese Emperor, and the requested sacred oil from the Holy Sepulcher. When granted audience with the Emperor, they presented the sacred oil from Jerusalem and the Papal letters—but they had failed to present the requested one hundred learned men to instruct the Chinese in Christianity and the Seven Arts of Western Culture.

Kublai Khan was less than pleased by this failure to present the Western learned men, and declined the Polos' request to leave China. However, they still proved useful to his Highness by sharing their experience and extensive knowledge of the peoples, kingdoms, and cultures they had passed through to reach his Court. Marco would later travel extensively throughout the Mongol Empire. Some historical scholars suspect he possibly served as one of the Great Khan's officials.

In 1292, the Polos left China by sea on a three-year journey of further adventures and dangers, arriving back in Venice with the treasures and wealth that had been their purpose. Their city was at war at the time, with the rival Italian trading city of Genoa. Marco joined the fray, but was captured in a sea battle, and while held in prison, immortalized his fantastic journey and place in history. He dictated the detailed accounts of his travels to a fellow inmate named Rustichello da Pisa, a romance writer, who incorporated stories of his own alongside other tales about current affairs of China.

Their co-written book, The Travels of Marco Polo, spread throughout Europe in manuscript form, and was the West's first comprehensive publication about the cultures of the Far East. Due to this astounding journey's rich descriptions of the foreign lands, peoples, and adventures, the story lived on to help reshape world history. Europe and its people shifted, were inspired, and broke out of the Middle Ages into the Renaissance, and the Modern Age to follow. Christopher Columbus himself had a copy of the book with handwritten annotations among his private possessions.

The first telephone call I made the morning after our return was to my own parents. I reported myself and their grandson safely back home and we arranged a time to stop by for the sharing of photographs and stories. Shortly after the call, while in the midst of errands, HondaCar failed to revive and had to be repaired yet again. Though the repair was inexpensive and only took a couple of extra hours, visions of securing a new vehicle then became a powerful commitment.

Though delayed, the reception from my parents later that afternoon was one of considerably entertainment and satisfaction. Mom and Dad extended very enthusiastic attentions and congratulations, saying, "We're glad you weren't eaten by bears!"

Those nearest and dearest to us express the most authentic interest in vacation stories, even if not told well. This one, with my photographic visual aids probably was one of my better efforts. We also brainstormed an interesting question: *Who was the specific person named McGuire that the mountain was named after?* Inquiries made while in Idaho had revealed nothing except shrugged shoulders and dumbfounded expressions. Speculating possibilities, three ideas were conjured.

Dad mentioned the McGuire Sisters, a 1940s pop music group, who were close to his heart while overseas. I offered Marc McGwire, the professional baseball player, but he spelled his name differently. Mountains do tend to be named after important men of legend or accomplishment, to be so honored. Presidents are popular namesakes for mountains, or the explorers who discovered them. We knew of no explorers with the name, nor presidents. Maybe a famous hero? Frederick Burnham has a mountain named after him, and Lord Baden-Powell has two!

On that possibility, my mother named a third candidate from the Second World War. A fighter pilot, he is credited with the second-highest number of air-combat victories for an American during the conflict. His name was Tommy McGuire. Hometown family and friends had nicknamed my mother "Tommy" when she was growing up, because of her tomboy conduct and sometimes aggressive behaviors of youth. Once Dad came along and they were married, she continued to go by Tommy, with McGuire now added. It was a great guess, and it seemed the most viable option. His is a compelling biography.

Thomas Buchanan McGuire, Jr. was born on August 1st, 1920, exactly ten months after my dad. He was raised by his mother in Sebring, Florida with the bio not mentioning his own father being present. He was in his third year of college at Georgia Tech when the Second World War came to America, and he joined the Army Air Corps in 1941.

Initially stationed in Alaska, Tommy flew patrol missions over the Aleutian Islands for a year, gaining experience and flying skills, but saw no combat there. McGuire was reassigned to the 475th Fighter Group of the Fifth Air Force in 1943, which was part of General McArthur's South Pacific command, and he soon entered battle with a vengeance.

On August 18th, Thomas was flying a Lockheed P-38 Lightning fighter aircraft on a bomber support mission over Wewak, New Guinea, when the group came under attack by Japanese intercepting fighters. In his first dogfight, he shot down three enemy fighter planes. The next day, on another support mission, he shot down two more Japanese interceptors and became a flying ace in just two days. McGuire's aviation, combat, and leadership skills did not go unrecognized, and he was promoted to the rank of Major and gained increased command authority. As his air victories increased, so did his fame, and his name was soon a regular feature in the newspapers. Charles Lindberg, the famous aviator first to fly an aircraft over the Atlantic Ocean, even came over from the States to fly a few unauthorized missions with Tommy. It's claimed Lindberg shot down an enemy plane on one of those flights.

McGuire also demonstrated nearly outrageous courage in the face of the enemy, once attacking seven enemy aircraft alone to assist a comrade in trouble. Though he shot down three of the enemy, the other four severely damaged his own aircraft and forced him to bail out, which almost killed him, as his parachute became ensnared in the cockpit. Freeing himself at the last moment, the chute had barely deployed before he landed in the water of Oro Bay, New Guinea. Bleeding from a large-calibre bullet wound to the wrist and suffering from several broken ribs, he was fortunately saved from the shark-infested water by a PT-boat. Tommy was hospitalized for six weeks before returning to his unit and was awarded the Purple Heart and Silver Star medals for gallantry.

My own father served in New Guinea, and repeatedly mentions the miserable monsoon-rain weather conditions, roads of mud, and insects that tortured the American soldiers there. Nearly a third of the troops serving in that theater were struck down by heat, malaria, dysentery, chronic fevers, obscene skin rashes, trench foot, and a host of other bugs, reptiles, and diseases. The running joke with his brother is that he got the crap detail and my uncle got the champagne. Dad's younger brother had enlisted, proven a proficiency for codes, and served in the war well behind the combat lines in an intelligence unit headquarters of the European Theater, describing it as, "the lap of luxury."

Flying Ace Tommy McGuire was not immune to nature either, and it's said that if he had not been burdened by periodic jungle illnesses and an ever-growing administrative workload he might well have set the record for enemy combat aircraft kills, and become the top American fighter ace of WWII. It was not to be, however. During a mission over Negros Island in the central Philippines in early January 1945, his plane crashed and exploded in the ocean during a dogfight with enemy aircraft. His score of thirty-eight was two victories short of the American record holder of that war, Major Richard Bong. His government awarded him, posthumously, the U.S. Medal of Honor, which, alongside his other awards, made him one of the most decorated Americans of the war. He lived twenty-four years and five months.

***

Everyone was quite proud of Justin, especially his Uncles Rob and Chuck, who had revisited their own Scouting days in adulthood as Scoutmasters. They made great mention of being impressed with the fact that he was still on good terms with their eldest brother. Rob and a third brother, Uncle Bill, had contributed several items to the excursion. After viewing the photographs, they even expressed interest in taking on the mountain themselves with my son, provided I was not part of the expedition. Each had a list of evidences that the biggest challenge was putting up with Justin's father, a most probable impossibility. Some sibling grudges run long and die hard. The bandwagon would stay empty, and in the end, the participants of our next trip west would be the same father-son duo.

"Yes, ladies and gentlemen, behind curtain number one is a brand-new car!"

Applause! Music!

It was a dark candy red Ford Ranger 4x4 pickup truck with an extended cab, oversized off-road tires, automatic transmission, plush interior, multidisc CD player, with fog running lights. No

120

more old, small, wimpy, hesitant, wheels-nearly-falling-off vehicle for next year. This first item from our "What Worked and Didn't Work" list was researched and handled methodically, naturally with accompanying reluctant banks, car salesmen, and income-thinning car payments. Indiana has no TV gameshows except the lottery, and my numbers never came up so I quit buying the tickets. But I was determined to spare no expense to swiftly put transportation on the "No Surprises" list.

The second major item was to teach Justin how to drive a manual transmission vehicle. Justin's year working with me had put some very decent money in the greedy hands of my teenager, and as predicted, money plus mobility had taxed the use of his mother's car as his own agenda expanded. She was wanting to buy him an inexpensive vehicle for his exclusive use, though admittedly just a clunker. With my own purchase accomplished and the HondaCar once again in running condition, it made sense that Justin use my cast-off until he'd saved money enough for his own acquisition. And so it was that I fulfilled on my promised second driving lesson.

With trepidation Justin again sat in the HondaCar driver's seat, and once again in a mostly empty shopping mall parking lot. The car had stalled after the mandatory "Ride 'em, cowboy!" bucking and jerk-to-a-stop following his inexperienced coordination of gas pedal and clutch. For some reason, while on the road in Sioux City and until this moment, I had forgotten to share with him the best trick for identifying the clutch-gas pedal "sweet spot." I now belatedly did this. "Close your eyes, Son, and keep them closed." He complied.

"Depress the clutch and start the engine."

He depressed the clutch, turned the ignition key, and the engine roared.

"Keep your eyes closed and rev the engine back and forth to the point you remember the sound being at the correct pitch. Listen for the sweet spot."

Justin practiced revving to different pitches between the idle whisper and roaring for about 30 seconds.

"Now rev the engine to about a third…that's it, that's right. Now slowly let out the clutch…keep your eyes closed. I'm watching for you and I'll tell you if something is close. It is all clear ahead… close your eyes."

The car slipped in gear and smoothly moved forward perfectly to about fifteen miles per hour.

"You've done it Justin! Now open your eyes and try second gear…and turn a little to the right."

He completed the operation flawlessly and away we went, tooling all around the parking lot.

After having him stop and restart again, he again achieved a flawless performance and the automobile became his.

Justin would now be able to work, socialize, and perhaps even assist with household transportation needs. If the school grades held up, he would be more independent. His academic performance had been a much-appreciated bright spot since he had begun his martial arts training, which he still kept his hand in from time to time. That discipline had dramatically centered him, helped form him into a generous, self-assured, authentically friendly, and a gentle young man. Everyone got on well with him to the point of broad, complimentary comments and praises. He was now in a pretty good groove, and hopes were high that with his now independent mobility, this apparent maturity would continue to flourish, with continued good outcomes.

***

Justin and I proceeded on to working and planning together over the intervening months for Road Trip Two. It now became a passion as we acquired new equipment, accouterment, and forecast an itinerary of grand adventure. The constraints of time were expanded, with one new exciting and novel wilderness exploration activity to be included. That activity was a guided whitewater rafting through the very heart of the Frank Church Wilderness. We would raft five days, tent camp four nights, and pass directly by our Namesake Mountain at its lowest geographical base. Additionally, we would forgo the backpacking and employ a professional wilderness outfitter. The outfitter would ferry us and our camping gear by horseback to a place near the mountain and back. At least three days would be available to figure out the logistics and plausibility of the climb.

As summer turned to autumn, Justin had been experiencing new vehicular mobility, but he was also picking up extra shifts at the restaurant we worked at. I became concerned that he was missing soccer practices and possibly letting his grades slip. When I confronted him about these concerns, he finally disclosed the news that he'd been cut from the soccer team. He did mention disappointment, but also optimism that perhaps it was for the best. Justin still had occasional martial arts participation, and the extra money he more than enjoyed earning. He would also continue participating with his school track team in the spring. Later conversation with his mother allayed my fears that he was drifting, and concerns of trouble on the horizon were put aside as this new status quo was now adopted.

Baden-Powell was in favor of boys earning their own ways to support their new Scouting activities:

"Boys are not too young to work for money."

"A great amount of poverty and unemployment results from boys being allowed to run riot outside the school walls as loafers, or from being used early in life as small wage-earners…"

They could earn their way, he suggested, by making walking sticks or sets of buttons, breeding canaries, beekeeping, chopping bundles of firewood, making nets, keeping goats and selling their milk, pottery-making, bookbinding, tending a garden and selling vegetables, and forming a minstrel troupe.

One of the first Scout Merit Badges, in fact, was basketry—not so much for art, but as an income-generating skill.

Many of my childhood visits to the small, rural village of Dover, Indiana, where my mother was born and where my grandparents still lived, were taken accompanying my Aunt Elvie on her weekend trips there. She would regularly look in on her parents and visit other relatives and friends. Elvie had never married, preferring being single, working as an insurance executive's secretary in our city, and basically free to run her own life simply, without complication of children and husband. Her two sisters had married and had become what some called "baby factories," birthing seven children each. Elvie's maternal instincts were more than satisfied by taking me and one or two of my brothers or cousins out of the city for an overnight with our Grandparents in the country. It served as a big pressure release for her sisters and us kids from the daily grind.

On one of these weekend excursions on a narrow, winding country road close to our destination, we passed by a road marker. It was a weathered and worn iron placard that she stopped at for my brother John and me to view. It was here that my lifelong interest in history was born.

"This sign says that it was on this road that 'General John Hunt Morgan and his Terrible Men' passed by on their Great Raid in the northern states!" my aunt exclaimed.

"Was he a good guy?" my brother asked.

"Why were his men terrible?" I further questioned.

"He was a Confederate general in the American Civil War a hundred years ago. The terrible men were his Rebel Army, and they were terrible because they robbed and stole from the people who lived here at the time. They robbed and ransacked the general store of your great-great-grandfather, James Murtaugh, in Dover!"

"Did they hurt him?" brother John inquired.

"Not very much. They say the rebel soldiers roughed him up pretty good when he complained that they weren't paying for the whiskey they were drinking," she answered with a laugh.

In 1863, it was common for outlying general stores in small, rural villages where no tavern operated, to stock a keg of whiskey for retail consumption. Sold by the one-ounce drinking shot for five cents, it was considered a customary and good service to the local farmers and working men. Otherwise, the sometimes "thirsty" customer would have to walk or travel by his tired workhorse three or four miles to the next nearest town tavern. And, I'm sure my great-great-grandfather realized that his usually frugal customers might be more inclined to purchase an extra luxury item occasionally while "under the influence." His general store carried everything from food, soap, and clothing and fabrics by the roll, to tools, hammers, and nails.

"Then," Elvie continued, "as the drunken soldiers ransacked his whole store, they took what they pleased, breaking and smashing everything else. They took the big bolts of cloth fabric that folks of that time used to make their own clothes from, and unrolled them while riding their horses, dragging them down the muddy road. That's why your great-great-grandfather became the most famous man in the town!"

In fact, James Murtaugh did thrive after the war. He built a solidly large, redbrick home that still stands today and is on the State registry of historic homes. He is also remembered with one of the largest gravestones in the village cemetery. With this background, it is little wonder that one of my favorite pleasures is in the reading of history. Great stories of mostly nonfiction? That's what I like to believe, anyway. Regardless, the story of my great-great-grandfather does survive in a recent history book about General Morgan's Great Raid of 1863, which is quite the interesting tale itself.

CHAPTER
NINE

Summer, 1997

Road Trip Two, Day One…

Day one of Father-Son Road Trip Two was even more meticulously planned and prepared for, but the demon gate keepers of the Human Life Activity Groove again would not allow easy escape from our hometown. In fact, the grooves proved to be ruts, once again full of the sticky, muddy muck emitting very thick mind-fog. We didn't reach the highway until 4:30 P.M., an even later start than the year before.

Following the summer evening sun at last, our new truck effortlessly cruised along at seventy-two miles per hour while the quad-speaker CD player filled the cabin with the Steve Miller Band: *"Time keeps on slippin', slippin', slippin'…into the future."* The air conditioner cooled my heated temper, stoked hot by the day's earlier thwarted intentions, as we ate our long-belated roast beef sandwich lunches. This replay of running late would have us pushing to make up for the time delays, but settling for Iowa City would prove sufficient this day—and it was the same motel as the previous year that we revisited for the night.

Justin and I had spent time during our preplanning again identifying specific "side trip" options that we thought would be fun, interesting, and easily taken-in while traveling west. With new, dependable wheels and familiarity of the route, sites for extra camping, motels, and investigations could happen and still cover the distance in four days with ample time to spare. Team driving would assure plenty of rest, so energies would be in surplus for Yellowstone National Park and the Grand Tetons which beckoned. Custer's Last Stand at the Little Big Horn, and even the Black Hills Gold Rush attractions were of keen interest.

Gold is a chemical element with the symbol Au and has the atomic number 79. It is a bright yellow, dense, soft, malleable, and ductile metal and these properties remain when exposed to air or water. Chemically, gold is a transition metal and a Group 11 element, and is one of the least reactive. Therefore, the metal occurs often as nuggets or grains in rocks, in veins, and in alluvial deposits. This metal has been a valuable and highly sought-after precious commodity for coinage, jewelry, and other arts since long before the beginning of recorded history.

Gold is mentioned very early in the Old Testament of the Hebrew and Christian Bibles.

Quote from the King James version of Genesis, Chapter Two, Verse 11: *"And the name of the first (river) is Pison: that is it which compasseth the whole land of Havilah, where there is gold..."* Verse 12: *"And the gold of that land is good: there is bdellium (crystal) and onyx stone."*

It strikes me as being of great interest that these words from mankind's creator characterize gold and where to find it, as well as precious stones, before getting around to creating a woman. That doesn't happen until some nine verses later.

After having man name all the cattle of the fields, birds of the air, and every other living creature (as well as what to eat and what not to eat), man is put to work... in a garden?

Or was that "garden" just a botanically decorated hole in the ground where the first man was put to work digging for gold and precious stones? For who? There aren't any other men around yet to bribe, buy from, or trade with.

Was God really a female, attracted to bright, shiny things? Was it a She who is the real boss of the universe?

Oh, and the part regarding what man is not to eat, Verse 17: *"But of the tree of the Knowledge of good and evil, thou shalt not eat of it; for in the day that thou eatest thereof thou shalt surely die."* (Translation: *"If ya break the rule, yer gonna git kilt."* ...or...There are consequences for breaking the rules!)

Finally, at Verse 21, man (Adam) is put to sleep, and one of his ribs is removed, the flesh closed up, and the rib is then made (incubated?) into a woman. Ouch! That probably wasn't pleasant to wake up to. When Adam awoke, he saw the woman and named her Eve...but he was probably just groaning, requesting the "evening darkness" to aid his return to sleep and make the pain go away.

So, there they were, butt naked together, cleaving to each other and becoming one in the Garden of Paradise, eating and drinking and having fun at work and play.

Really?

If farming is so much fun, why do most farm girls move to the city? It's a well-known fact that a woman tends to be more street-smart than a man, and Eve had some leverage with all that "cleaving together" stuff.

So maybe Adam was a stubborn cuss who wasn't too sharp. It takes a stubborn man to prospect for gold, because it's usually found in rocks... hard, brittle rocks, and not very often... hard labor... very tedious.

Maybe Eve decided to give Adam the forbidden fruit from the tree of knowledge so he would quit digging up rocks all day and night and pay her more attention. Maybe she wanted him to take her on vacation by the beach... have shellfish for a change of pace with the menu... and dance under the stars. Eden had a beach, right? It *was* Paradise, after all.

Poor things... they were just human... imperfect, we're told... and like most people, wanting a better life and not realizing what they already had... but, I digress...

Gold artifacts found at the Nahal Qana (Kana) cave cemetery, which were dated by archeologists during the 1980s, showed these to be from within the Chalcolithic period, and is considered the earliest find of gold from the Levant.

...The Nahal Qana is an intermittent stream in Israel and begins in the hills of Mount Gerizim.

...The Chalcolithic period was the first part of the Bronze Age, dating from 5,000 BCE.

"Yes, sir, there be gold in them hills..."

The first North American Gold Rush occurred in Cabarrus County, North Carolina, in 1803, when a bunch of gold seekers' claims were made around a farm owned by John Reed. His son had found an interesting seventeen-pound yellow rock in Little Meadow Creek, which passed through the property. For three years that rock served as a doorstop and conversation piece. A jeweler from Fayetteville identified the rock as a large gold nugget in 1799, and told John to name his price. Reed had no understanding of the true value of gold, but he figured a week's worth of wages was a great deal for a doorstop. He demanded $3.50 for his rock. The true value at that time was $3,600.

It really is all about what one allows his eyes to be educated to see.

John Reed had been educated by this event and organized a small gold-mining operation, ultimately finding enough wealth to die a rich man. So much gold was found in the area that the Charlotte Mint was built in nearby Charlotte, North Carolina, in the year 1835 to handle it all. The first government assessor of that mint was the father of General John Gibbon, of the American Civil War and western frontier Indian wars fame. During the American Civil War, the Confederacy has often been portrayed to be well supplied with gold bullion; many myths and legends still abound of undiscovered Confederate gold treasure being stashed, buried, and hidden away, only awaiting discovery. The Reed Gold Mine was one productive source and would continue operating until 1912. It is now a state historic site with a museum. A few of the mining tunnels have been refurbished and are now a tourist attraction available to be viewed.

Day Two...

An early morning start on day two held great promise for making up some of the time lost with our delayed departure, as the only threatening impediment appeared to be the minor slowing of road constructions and repairs. The route we had chosen was much less traveled within the Interstate network, so traffic was no hindrance. Thus, the miles flew by us as my son shared the driving effort in competent manner (despite my occasional comments about minding the posted speed limits and the displeasure his rap music gave me). Traffic and construction congestions of Des Moines, Sioux City, and Sioux Falls proved little delay, and only long after crossing the Missouri River, where a violent summer storm was encountered, did any of the driving mirror the previous year's drama.

The "Big Sky" view of a prairie from a rest stop revealed the fast-approaching weather front coming at us from the northwest. Confident in the four-wheel drive of our vehicle, we decided to join the other unintimidated drivers and push on through. We were not far from the Badlands National Park, had at least a couple more hours of daylight, and hoped to camp there for the night. The rain began splattering the windshield as we pulled out to the road, and the intensity grew until our speed had to be reduced. The sky turned black as midnight with periodic, bright, cracking streaks of lightning accompanied by deep rumbles of thunder that drowned out our music. High winds buffeted the Ranger, but the four-wheel drive traction was solid, and we even passed slower-moving vehicles when visibility would permit.

After about thirty minutes, the rain began to let up and the gusts of wind retreated. Once the rain stopped altogether, the Ranger was dry by the time we were pulling into our destination for the night. The dusk-darkened landscape was hidden by shadows, so little of the famed panorama could be discerned as we crept into the camping area. By that fading light our campsite was selected and shelter raised. A whole organic chicken was grilling over fired coals before twilight took over entirely.

Our camping area had been missed by the storm, but a gentle rain from a secondary, quieter cloud front began falling as our entrée neared cooked perfection. We moved into our tent to eat the succulent, warm, and juicy meat off the bone, complemented by baked beans, potato salad, slaw, and a couple of beers. The new Gaz compressed-fuel lantern supplied perfect light and a bit of warmth against the damp chill of the weather, and we laid back to browse some recreational reading before sleep time.

Finally lying at rest, just before dozing off, I listening to the prairie breeze and light rain whip around the tent. My mind imagined the sounds to be the whispers of ancient shaman spirits, still a presence of that land, chanting some kind of ritual, a possible blessing, perhaps a warning, or even a curse. Pondering those thoughts were my last before sleep.

Day Three...

The Badlands of southwestern South Dakota allow one to view and touch millions of years of geological, environmental, and biological transformations, so folks from all over the world visit this National Park to do just that every year. The history of the nearby Black Hills is also very compelling, with a multiplicity of stories, history, and tall tales that intrigue and entertain.

Thoughts upon rising on day three were preoccupied with more immediate matters, however, like coffee, a well-rounded and quick breakfast, and a smooth, early getaway to our next destination of Stanley, Idaho. Visiting some of the Black Hills' attractions and taking in a scenic drive of the Badlands invited also. Allowing Justin to sleep in an extra half hour, I sat alone at sunrise with my hot morning beverage in quiet contemplation. Admiring the surrounding rugged landscape of sharply eroded buttes, pinnacles, and spires that surrounded our camp area, I casually observed as our neighboring campers began their own rituals of daybreak.

Being a people watcher from way back, it was inevitable that pieces and bits of conversation were overheard, and the agendas of our camp neighbors that I could decipher illustrated the variety of adventures nearby. A group directly adjacent to us was planning to hike the Fossil Exhibit Trail that day, which is led daily by a park volunteer. Over seventy-five-million-years' worth of fossils are viewable within this park, and they tangibly demonstrate the evolution of life on the planet. The Badlands contain one of the most prodigious and accessible evidentiary continuums of ancient fossilized animal and plant life in the world, dating back deep into the Mesozoic Era when dinosaurs ruled the earth and seas. In fact, the entire area was at one time an inland sea with all sorts of monsters swimming about while giant reptiles crawled and dinosaurs trotted along the seashore, probably on the run from the stalking Tyrannosaurus Rex.

As the tectonic plates shifted and volcanic eruptions of the Rocky Mountains and Black Hills uplifted the area, the sea had drained away. An extinction event wiped out the dinosaurs and the rock tells the story of what followed in some detail, to when mammals appeared and dominated. The rock spires, eroded mountains, and hillsides reveal sedimentary deposit layers of rock formed by successional eras of tropical forests, open woodlands, meandering rivers, and floodplains. Giant bears, miniature horses, woolly mammoths, and saber-toothed cats roamed and hunted the area, leaving behind their skeletal remains. Finally, in the last few speckles of sand within the evolutionary hourglass, ancient tribes of men appeared. The stone spearheads of Clovis Man and/or some other Proto-Amerindian tribes have been found near there.

Studies of Amerindian oral histories disclose that the area was populated by the Arikara Indian tribe from about the twelfth century until the early eighteenth century, when the Teton Sioux tribes pushed them out and father north. It was the Sioux who introduced the name "The Badlands." The Sioux Indian Pine Ridge Reservation is south of the 244,000-acre park and designated wilderness section, and they help administrate and care for the land and wildlife here. Another group of neighboring campers were headed in that direction to check out the Wounded Knee Memorial, site of the last big bloodletting between that tribe and the U.S. Army in 1890.

I overheard a third group from Chicago planning a bicycling day expedition through the park, intent on photographing the diverse wildlife (of which there are some thirty-nine mammal species, including free-roaming bison, antelope, and prairie dog colonies). There are also over two hundred bird species observable. The posted signs had already given warning of rattlesnakes, and there are eight other reptile species inhabiting the park, but I've not been a fan of reptiles since my pet box turtle bit me when I was a kid. For the butterfly enthusiast, the park advertises sixty-nine different species, and even six different amphibians for the real biology lovers. Seeing some bison on the open range would be cool enough, as far as I was concerned.

Once Justin rose from his rest, we proceeded with our own morning activities: eating, cleaning up, and packing for the next leg of travel. Just as we were finishing the third repacking of the truck, I noticed with alarm that a rear tire looked very low on air. Closer inspection confirmed that the tire was indeed seriously underinflated by more than half, so now the day would take on a new complexion. My response to this fly in the ointment did at least stay muted, muttered cussing of mild nature being my calming strategy. There was a town just a couple of miles away that surely would have road services that could fix the damn thing, I told my son. We finished packing, I consulted the road map, and off we went to what appeared the most likely avenue to the town.

Get Real. Murphy's Law was in full throttle as we made our way along the scenic byway…in the wrong direction.

After driving something close to fifteen minutes, my brain said, *This don't feel right. The town should have shown up by now, even at our reduced speed.*

Only more high-traffic scenic roadway with fellow tourist vehicles were in view, twisting and turning through the hills of the park, overlooking the sterile, desolate, and forbidding landscape of the valley below and ghostly mountains beyond. Once I'd officially concluded that we were absolutely headed the wrong way, the road itself conspired to frustrate corrective action. The two-lane highway offered no pull-over/turn-around areas for another ten slow-motion minutes. A long line of oncoming traffic, coupled with an equally long line of traffic behind me, dissuaded attempting a three-point turnaround. Meanwhile, the tire was sinking flatter by the second and we would soon be riding the wheel rim.

At long last, a large scenic overlook parking area appeared, where a course correction was accomplished easily. Back down into the valley we inched, with hazard lights blinking, finally reaching our point of previous departure and a big sign with a clear arrow pointing us to the town of Interior, two miles away. In nine minutes, we had reached one of the two gas stations of this very small community, and we were greeted cordially by a man who looked as Native American Indian as a person could. Dark red/sunburn complexion, jet-black eyes and hair in a short ponytail, the lean and well-muscled man was wearing a pale-yellow cowboy hat, cowboy boots, blue jeans, and a checkered red and blue shirt with a white neckerchief. He was about my age, with graying temples and a western drawl that would make John Wayne proud.

"Can anyone here help me fix a tire going flat?" I asked him as he walked up to our hobbled Ranger.

"Yeah, I imagine so," he responded with assurance.

"How much will it cost me?" I asked, a smile taking over my expression.

"Oh, twelve dollars ought to cover the trouble," he answered, smiling right back.

"You're on," I chuckled, much relieved.

"My name is Bill, but I'm not so wild any more. Take a seat in the shade while I get this done," he said with a dry humor.

Justin and I exited the vehicle and moved under an outdoor awning that shaded a bench. The tire puncture had obviously occurred the day before, which was Day Two of this journey. Our break-down of the previous year had also occurred the second day on the road. Coincidence? Very weird. Was there something more to that whispering wind and rain outside my tent the night before that had played so vividly and strangely with my imagination?

The late-morning sun moved past the eleventh hour of the day, and our time was passed talking with Not-So-Wild-Bill, as he fixed our tire puncture, about our destination and mission. He expressed a lot of interest and even asked for follow-up details. He shared that he hoped to do something similar with one of his own sons someday. In about a ten-minute jiffy, the tire was repaired and good as new. The large nail that had inflicted a puncture the previous day was removed, the hole plugged, patched, and his modest fee paid. Bill wished us luck, and we were again heading down the byways of America to complete the Badlands Scenic Highway Loop Road prematurely started.

My earlier impressions of a "sterile" and foreboding environment transformed into an otherworldly sense of new freedom, bright with color and teaming with life as we passed wild prong-horned deer and antelope grazing in the distance, while flocks of birds also appeared active and numerous. Stopping halfway to enjoy magnificent panoramas and snap some obligatory tourist photos was also indulged, even though we knew full well that the photographs could not do justice to the geologic spectacle that are the Badlands. Examination of a nearby eroded hillside revealed horizontal, colored stripes of rock that clearly identified each passing epoch of time…when the dinosaurs lived and died out, when the early mammals appeared, and later inherited the earth.

Weird, giant mammals like a beast known as the Brontothere, a four-legged creature standing eight feet tall, who is thought to have roamed in packs on this land. He was thick-skinned and bodied, weighed four thousand pounds, and was a distant relative of the rhinoceros, but with two elongated snout horns and a more volatile personality. Continuing our climb out of the remains of that ancient inland sea, it was easy to imagine groups of massive mammoths, dire wolf packs, and the three-hundred-pound, vicious, pig-like Platygonus.

The jagged peaks of the mountains were soon all that was visible as we navigated up through the treeless landscape to the National Grassland Preserve, where huge herds of American bison had once grazed. The animals could often weigh up to one thousand pounds and were very agile, sometimes running at thirty-five miles per hour and jumping up to six feet high. Stalked by the pre-Columbian Indian tribes who inhabited the Great Plains, the beast was difficult and dangerous, and hunting it required grassfires and herding stampedes over cliffs. This technique was unpredictable for success, however, and the bison really had very few other predator dangers, so it thrived. An estimated sixty million animals roamed North America prior to 1492, ranging from the far northwest of Canada, down to Mexico, over to the Atlantic Seaboard of New York, and down to Georgia (as far as Florida, by some sources). Two huge mega herds were still west of the Mississippi River in 1800, thought to have up to fifty million bison between them.

In the 1500s the horse was reintroduced to central North America. Several tribes of Native Americans soon were mastering the arts of equestrianism and husbandry, notably the Comanche, Cheyenne, Nez Perce, and the Teton Sioux. This new animal transformed life for these tribes from that of a stone-age primitive subsistence to a lifestyle approaching "freedom from want." The horse empowered people with an exponential increase in mobility. The abundant bison could and would be harvested, at will, because these tribes could now migrate with them. The harvest would yield a large proportion of the material needs of the tribes, providing durable hides for shelter and clothing, bones for tools and camp implements, and protein-rich, lean meat for sustenance. The Indians of the Great Western Plains were to develop a new and powerful culture of nomadic freedom, often described as "idyllic," over the next three hundred years.

The plan that Justin and I had forecast for this day had suffered delay enough that our itinerary required adaptation. We had hoped to proceed onward and investigate the mining town of Deadwood in the nearby Black Hills…perhaps check out the gambling saloon where the famed gunslinger Wild Bill Hickok met his demise as he played poker, holding what is still called the "Dead Man's Hand" of "Aces and Eights." A visit to Boot Hill where the remains of Calamity Jane, Wild Bill Hickok, and other colorful characters of the time now lay at rest sounded kinda cool. The great mountain sculptures of Mount Rushmore and Chief Crazy Horse, bypassed the previous year, would've been awesome to see. Even a tour of the Homestake Mining Company Museum in the adjacent town of Lead could have been interesting, where that special substance called gold was still being extracted.

Approaching the Interstate access, yet one more highly

advertised attraction lay before us. Wall Drug was offering a cup of coffee for a nickel, and after the travails and fortunes of that day already, the idea of a quick coffee break sounded deliciously welcome. The town of Wall even had a huge, eighty-foot-tall model of a green Apatosaurus surrounded by colored flags. Large and clear signage directed us through the small community to a main commercial area overflowing with vehicles and people. We beheld what could be one of the largest tourist traps ever conjured, with dozens of storefronts selling clothing and footwear, eateries and saloons, with the famous Wall Drug Store at the center.

The famous Wall Drug

Amongst all of the hustle and bustle, we surprisingly found parking with ease, so into the Mecca of Cheap Consumerism we plunged, in search of that five-cent cup of coffee.

A second, bigger surprise greeted us as we entered the large building. The lobby of Wall Drug is a rustic, well-finished wood interior that contains one of the best western art museums in the country. As one walks through, various hallways split off to where a score of small shops form a cowboy-themed department store. The five-cent coffee stand was eventually located as Justin and I slowly walked through the hallways, viewing old pioneer, cowboy, Indian, and homesteader photographs, as well as reading short stories about the local and greater area's history.

When I asked where to pay for the coffee, one of the passing employees said, "You really don't have to pay."

I insisted that I felt it was a required ritual, considering the price.

"If you must, just leave it on the coffee service table."

That's what I did, and with the nickel clinking onto the tabletop, I thanked the guy for his assistance.

We moved on, joining the crowd of fellow tourists and purchased a few postcards. We also opted to do lunch at one of the eateries because the smell of sizzling steak sandwiches and fries was too appealing to pass up. After consuming our meals and on the way out, photos were taken of several wood-carved, life-sized figures of cowboys, Indians, and homesteaders in various pose. This "pit-stop" consumed two whole hours. It is easy to agree with author Bill Bryson's opinion of Wall Drug: "It's an awful place, one of the world's worst tourist traps, but I loved it and won't have a word said against it."

Departure from this place went smoothly, but the clock was ticking close to three by that time, so the journey was badly behind schedule. We had over one thousand miles to cover within the next twenty-eight hours. Stanley, Idaho was where we would meet with our river-rafting group, and the orientation meeting was scheduled for six o'clock the next evening. Further side explorations needed to be deferred until our return trip, eating miles now being our critical mission.

With some regret, the Ranger sped by the historical battlefields, towns of interest and lore, and other geographical sites of stories and legends. Once again, we passed through the Black Hills, the prairies, and by the Bighorn Mountains of Wyoming. Soon after driving through the Crow Indian Reservation, we approached Billings, Montana after the sun was well down. Justin had helped with the driving chores, but I found my nerves too on edge to dare resting my eyes with my son at the helm. Nevertheless, our energies were still strong enough to bypass Billings as our stop for the evening, and we pushed on about two more hours. We ran completely out of steam around midnight. All that was available at this point was a nearly full highway rest stop. We slept about five hours in the Ranger, though there were several short interruptions. The extended cab was still a very tight space, with no real room to stretch out within. Periodic noise from sporadic commercial truck traffic prevented deep sleep.

Day Four...

Several motor vehicles starting their engines and exiting the parking area woke us into a damp and chilly dawn. Morning frost covered the windshield. Stiff muscles from our cramped sleep accommodations encouraged movement, so the public restroom served as an inviting excuse to get up and moving before breakfasting on fruit juice and sandwiches from our travel cooler. Justin took an unusually longer time dealing with his morning constitutionals, so it was about forty minutes before we got underway, with a bright sun breaking clear of the eastern horizon. I also took exception with his driving this morning, which resulted in his refusal to continue if I couldn't tolerate his penchant to exceed the posted eighty-mile-per-hour speed limits. We switched seats. Silence was his response to my own muted chatter for the next three hours. The miles melted away faster than I had anticipated, so before nine o'clock we were well beyond the Interstate and retracing our path from the year before over to the Lost Trail Pass at the Continental Divide and the Montana-Idaho border.

On the road leading through the Beaverhead/Deerlodge National Forests and along the Big Hole River, I saw the car in front of us signal and turn into the Big Hole National Battlefield entrance. The site was open, even though it felt too early. Quite a few other vehicles could be seen in the parking area. Sharing this unexpected luck with Justin, I turned back to this missed attraction from last year. At least for me, this was to be a very satisfying side exploration, due to the largely simplified yet far-reaching historical story it is part of. That my son did not share my enthusiasm was another surprise. He accompanied me into the visitor's center and museum, did a quick walkthrough, declared the place "boring," and returned to the parking lot.

I continued my own investigations of the museum rooms, surrounded by artifact displays, photographs of the key personages of the event, and a short video of how the battle occurred. After about forty-five minutes, I moved to a bookstore and park administrative area where a few fellow patrons were perusing books, maps, tourist souvenir items, and speaking to a couple of park employees at a service counter. Awaiting my turn to buy a book about the conflict (*Chief Joseph's War*) I could overhear snippets of the conversations three of the folks ahead of me were having.

Two of them were a brother-sister pair seeking guidance in locating a specific area of the park where they believed their great-great-grandmother may've been buried—who happened to be one of the Indian women killed in the initial attack by the U.S. Army. The third was a single man simultaneously speaking with the second park employee, discussing his own ancestor, one of the white volunteers who also had died at this battle, asking how to find the exact spot where he may have fallen. It was an absolutely captivating experience. I listened as the participants gestured and pointed out a large bay window overlooking a portion of the Indian encampment area of the battleground. These were people with blood and skin in the game, so I was very pleased at the coincidental good fortune that I might share these moments of the present with them in this small way. It gave continued meaning to this patch of ground and what occurred here, illustrating just one of the many ways how deserving and important that memorial is.

This small area was the turning point of one of the last major military mobilizations and wars between the U.S. Army and the unassimilated Indians of the western frontier. The Nez Perce tribe, long dependably peaceful, had finally rebelled against continuous white encroachments on their treaty-guaranteed historic homelands. The Nez Perce record having occupied the lands of central Idaho and eastern Oregon since B.C.E. 6,000.

Some younger Indian warriors had struck back at the white settlers in June of 1877, killing several, and about 750 men, women, and children of the tribe decided to flee their tribal lands rather than surrender at the diminished reservation assigned to the Nez Perce. A new treaty had been struck by a small minority of "Christianized" tribal members, which was in contravention to the previous U.S. Government treaty agreements signed over twenty year before. Several deadly engagements followed as the Indians made their way across the Territory of Idaho toward Montana Territory, hoping to gain sanctuary there with the Crow Indian tribe. The pursuing U.S. military had come out second best with these new opponents at every turn, and the Indians felt naïve confidence that their situation was secure once camped at the Big Hole River. Once crossing out of Idaho, the principal leader of the Nez Perce, Chief Looking Glass, had pledged not to attack any of the white settlements as they moved at a more leisurely pace south and down the Bitterroot Valley. Along this path, they even traded and purchased supplies from white merchants. But there was still another deadly enemy closing in for a killing. John Oliver Gibbon served as a distinguished general during the American Civil War commanding troops in the Army of the Potomac, and fought in nearly every large battle until the surrender of the Confederacy. His first command as a general was fought so well, that his unit would be known as "The Iron Brigade," for their tenacity, stubbornness, and toughness. At Gettysburg, his division had stopped "Picket's Charge," key to winning the biggest battle of the war. Though wounded, General Gibbon recovered and served until the surrender of R.E. Lee's Army of Northern Virginia at Appomattox Courthouse in 1865.

Gibbon would continue in the Army after the war as a colonel, and by 1876, he was commanding a regiment in western Montana. His unit served as one of three primary combat forces attempting to force the Cheyenne and Sioux Indian tribes back onto their reservations in that year. The Indians defeated the other two military formations, and it was Col. Gibbon's men who rescued the surviving remains of Custer's 7th Cavalry at the Battleground of the Little Bighorn. They also buried the dead, mutilated, and desecrated soldiers there.

Colonel John Gibbon and two hundred soldiers and civilian volunteers were hot on the Nez Perce's trail, and the refugees were unaware of this hostile force as it charged, with guns blazing, in surprise attack on the morning of August 9th. Gibbon's orders to his command were simple—and savage: "We don't want any prisoners." Rushing into the village of eighty-nine tipis, the soldiers and militia fired into the tents of the sleeping Indians. The gunfire was indiscriminately aimed at the elderly, women, children, and warriors. Chaos ensued, and the Indians scattered in every direction. Whatever the shock and awe inflicted on the Nez Perce, confusion also soon devolved upon the attacking white Americans, and a halt was called to prevent the force from scattering. While the soldiers took time to burn the captured tipis, the Indian warriors reorganized and rallied. The Native Americans then started shooting back with effect.

The Nez Perce marksmanship was excellent: Gibbon's horse was shot down from under him and he was wounded in the leg.

One of his key subordinate leaders was killed, Lieutenant James Bradley, and the wing of men he commanded no longer conformed to plan. Judging his force outnumbered and position untenable, as several other soldiers around him were also shot and killed, Gibbon ordered retreat out of view of the village to where the white Americans dug rifle pits and constructed log barriers for defense. Actually, it was the whites who outnumbered the Nez Perce warriors, but the Indian sharpshooters battled aggressively and fired with deadly accuracy. Gibbon's men holed up for the rest of that day and the next with fears of being overrun and annihilated, like Custer the year before. On the second night, the Indians withdrew eighteen miles to the southeast. Gibbon's force was left behind, immobile and with little ammunition or water, and over a third of them killed or seriously wounded. Their only food was a dead horse.

Casualties for the Indians were also very grievous: between seventy and ninety dead, up to two-thirds being noncombatant old folks, women, and children. Nearly every Nez Perce family suffered loss in the battle. Chief Looking Glass lost prestige and Chief Joseph seems to have assumed the role as principal leader from that point. He would lead his people on an epic journey of more than one thousand miles, eluding pursuing U.S. military units of vastly superior numbers coming from all directions.

Further skirmishes occurred over the next two months as the Indian fugitives attempted escape through Montana to Canada, where they hoped to join the Sioux Tribe of Chief Sitting Bull. Finally, just forty miles short of their destination, the tribe was trapped and surrounded in the Bear Paw Mountains during a December snow storm. Many more had been killed and wounded during their long journey, the survivors having no food, and no winter blankets. The words spoken by Chief Joseph upon his surrender of his people has made him one of the iconic Native American Chiefs in history.

"... Hear me, my chiefs! I am tired; my heart is sick and sad. From where the sun now stands, I will fight no more forever."[20]

Finding my son standing outside next to our vehicle, I shared how great the exhibit was and questioned why he displayed such little interest. His answer, which I don't recall verbatim, reconfirmed his earlier statement of boredom with the entire

20 Beal, Merrill D

history topic. I was left wondering how I could have missed that attitude of his for so long. Perhaps it could have been a reaction to how much his uncles and I tended to drone on and on about history at family gatherings. It's probably not a popular topic to impress most high school girls with, I suppose.

Moving on up the road of the mountain, he shared that he felt it was a waste of time to be dawdling at some nearly unknown historical site while under pressure to be at a meeting by six o'clock that evening, some 400 miles away. We now had only eight hours. He did have a point, but had forgotten our clocks were ahead by an hour. I announced that we were finally "on time," and even ahead enough to have a great lunch at our favorite coffee shop and diner in Salmon, Idaho. He expressed slight relief, but something else seemed present on his mind that he wasn't divulging. I felt confident he would come around, blind to the possibility that he was down-right pissed at not being able to share the driving once again. This trip, my son would seem to be the one carrying extra baggage.

The lunch in Salmon was as good and relaxing as expected, and the chill in our relationship warmed considerably as the pangs in our stomachs eased. We headed out of town and soon spied the side road we would take to our Namesake Mountain, agreeing that there should be quite the contrast between ascending it and looking down, over one mile, at the river we were soon to journey, and raft right past it. Continuing up the Salmon River Valley to our destination within the Sawtooth Forest National Recreation Area, at the foot of the spectacular Sawtooth Mountains, it is about as scenic a drive as one could imagine. Further stops were taken to snap photos of dramatic compositions that road, river, huge rock, and the stunning vistas comprised, to fill our horizons. The quality was right up there with any National Geographic submission.

Though the last half of this final leg of our drive seemed to drag a bit as the National Forest closed in on the roadway from all sides, the open valley containing the town of Stanley was reached in good time. The motel reservations held up after a small initial confusion, and thirty minutes of lying out on the twin double beds in our room restored our stamina for what lie ahead. We met up for the all-important meeting with our guides and fellow customers in good time, the motel restaurant served us a fine meal, and we slept soundly until the wake-up call the following morning.

CHAPTER
TEN

Day Five...

Whitewater rafting began as a leisure sport in the 1970s and is most often done on river and creek whitewater to thrill the passengers. It is considered an extreme sport and can be very dangerous for injury, and even fatalities occur. The dangers have been greatly mitigated, however, due to the evolution and advances made in the durable and safe materials used for the rafts. Additionally, more people have become skilled in the river navigation arts as the sport has grown, such that many commercial companies are engaged in this recreational industry. Rafting trips are offered in lengths ranging from two hours to multiday journeys on the water, with skilled, professional guides ensuring a safe and exciting experience.

The degrees of rough water are measured in grades, from one to six. Grade I consists of mild water areas and requires very basic skill. While a Boy Scout, I had trained for and used both canoe and rowboat on such water and earned Merit Badges for each craft. My skills proved adequate for successfully navigating Grade II waters, which contained exposed and unexposed rocks, tree logs and large limbs, with sections of rough water that required practiced paddling. Grade III and IV rapids had faster and more dramatic rough waters, and require even greater expertise. Only the most expert rafters are allowed to attempt Grade V. Grade VI rapids are considered impassable.

The river we would be rafting, the Middle Fork Salmon, was rated Grades Two, Three, and even Four at this time of the year, depending on the changing monthly water volumes and sections being traversed. The Grade Four sections would involve negotiating considerably turbulent whitewater, substantial waves, large rocks, holes (depressions in the water ranging in depth of a few inches, to five-feet deep—not good to get one's raft trapped in), and require significant and exacting maneuvers by the guides and participants. The river gradient would be quite steep in spots as we would descend over three thousand feet during the adventure, taking a wet, aquatic roller coaster of sorts.

And you are going to get wet! As we found on river trip day one, the rubber wetsuits we saw for sale in town were offered for good reason. Our starting altitude was seven thousand feet—with snowcapped mountains in view—and even though the summer days got warm and sunny, the nights could get down into the thirty-degree range. There were still multiple spots of snow left over around the motel.

And the river was ice cold! Our raft-steering guide, Jake, made certain that we would enjoy (endure) every big freezing splash possible during the first two hours of river transit, starting at about ten o'clock in the morning. The raft was moving quite fast through what is described as a "rock garden" stretch of rapids the first hour, the declination at about forty feet per mile. There was water splashing onboard nearly every five minutes. The first Grade III+ rapids and Velvet Falls, was the first highlighted "attraction" that delivered a major drenching for the three passengers up front, two of them being Justin and myself. The bright summer sun provided very limited relief from the steady, brisk mountain breeze that amplified the chills on our water-soaked skin and clothing, and the shaded forest and canyon areas of the river provoked shivers. The break for lunch and an end to our initiation could not come soon enough.

Our first meal was not just a vast, varied, and delicious deli-styled spread, but also it allowed time to soak up the solar rays that dried our clothing and warmed up our chilled bodies. Upon re-boarding our raft some seventy-five minutes later, I politely mentioned to our guide that perhaps every large splash opportunity, particularly in the shaded areas of the river, didn't necessarily have to be indulged. My request was readily seconded by the other equally soaked and chilled participants sharing our ride. Thus, the next leg of our afternoon passage of the river was less rigorous, warmer, and provided time for conversation and acquaintance, photography of the awesome landscape, and brief observation of elk exposed among a thin stand of pine trees on a nearby hill.

There are three hundred ratable rapids on the Middle Fork Salmon River, at least twelve of which are Class III+ or Class IVs, and we were to run three of the big ones on this first day. Place-names of "Powerhouse" and "Pistol Creek" brought suspense to mind, especially as these next big splash obstacles drew near. Fortunately, our guide heeded the request for less of the ice-cold drama and steered to the softer edge of the river as we made the "run" of them (though we still did get wet). The sun had warmed the day by this time, however, the air fresh and dry, so water-soaked clothing dried quickly. We cheered, as did the entire group, after completion of those more tumultuous sections. It had been an exhilarating experience and all that was advertised.

Our rafting group was a fairly diverse crowd, ages ranging from ten to seventy-two years old, and split equally between male and female. There were six guides and about twenty other patrons. Our river guide team was quite extraordinary, an attractive squad of young men and women who excelled in every aspect while conducting our excursion through this magnificent wilderness. All were in strong physical condition, trained in Wilderness First Aid and Swift Water Rescue, and CPR certified. They were also great cooks, each contributing specialized recipes, and told entertaining stories of the area. They extended five-star hotel customer service.

When our guides weren't taking care of tenderfoot pilgrim thrill seekers during the summer, they had interesting lives. Two of the young men, Jake and Matt, were professional sportsmen. Both were single, had been river guiding for seven years or more, and worked as "Ski Patrol" for the skiing resorts in Utah and Jackson Hole, Wyoming, during the colder months. They had the longest experience and most of the stories to tell about the area.

The two female guides of the team were both the youngest and oldest of the squad. Susan was forty-two, lived in Idaho, was married to a truck driver, and also personally drove big-rig semi-trailer trucks nationwide in the off-season. She was very athletic and usually steered the group's paddle boat for those wanting more speed, whitewater bumps, extra thrills, and potential spills. Natalie was twenty-three, and this was her second summer working as a river guide, a journeywoman still training in the finer points of river navigation and raft management. She was single, also very athletic, and during the off-season her time was consumed with earning a master's degree in life sciences, if my memory serves me.

The two other male guides were of quieter personalities when I engaged them in conversation. George was a full-blooded Native

American who also spent his off-season as a university student studying mine engineering. The second young man, Josh, spent his winters crewing out of Alaska as a deep-sea fisherman on a small, six-man fishing vessel. Though a potentially lucrative occupation, it's also one of the most dangerous jobs in America. They were both also single. The guys were all in their late twenties or early thirties and were gentlemen of very high character. Each team member was most generous and friendly, making it their practice to provide special and individualized personal service to each rafter during the five-day trip. They were an extremely personable and professional crew.

River rafting utilizes a number of differently styled water craft, and our conveyances were of three different types. One was called a paddle raft, and it could accommodate up to eight paddling patrons, four on each side, with a guide in the rear to steer and command. A second craft was called an oar raft, which was larger and carried cargo and baggage, as well as customers desiring a more relaxed and observatory passage. A single guide would use large oars from the stern of the raft to navigate and propel the craft downriver at a more leisurely pace. The third craft type of our little flotilla were two inflatable kayaks used for single passage of the smaller rapids or for quiet fishing on more tranquil sections. Two wetsuits had also been brought along, since the kayaks immersed the body in the cold water for the entire time one might paddle about.

At about five o'clock in the evening, our river convoy made shore at our large, park-like campsite for the night. Tents, cots, and air mattresses were collected from one of the rafts, and we then paired off to select spots to raise our canvas sleeping rooms for the evening. After about an hour, folks followed wondrous aromas back to the common area where four of the guides were cooking foods with small portable camp stoves and Dutch ovens. But first, we were invited to a pre-dinner cocktail hour to better meet and greet, the chief guide distributing complimentary beer and wine (which the brochure had specified would not be provided). Camp chairs had been set up and arranged about the commons, so sitting or standing were options of choice as we did introductions, shared about the day and trip, and generally socialized and revitalized.

The meal that followed comprised steak with all the fixings, including hot breads, salads, steamed fresh veggies, and desserts.

Afterward, a campfire was set alight, and three or four of the group displayed decent talent with guitars and a harmonica. Others sang and hummed along. Everyone was invited to share jokes, stories, and what most impressed or disappointed them about the day. All was excitement without complaint. It was jovial and also intimate at times, and a bonding began forming among the group that seemed heartfelt and rare. As dusk passed and twilight came on, Justin and I left the party and moved to our tent, quite tired, ready to turn in for the night.

Of course, once settled and bedded down for more than a few minutes, nature did call me back, so I took one last walk to the camp-provided rest room. By then, the full dark of a moonless and chilling night was present over the now-quiet encampment. By flashlight my breath was visible as I picked a way across the ink-black, uneven ground, past two neighboring tents, one with dull light seeping out. On the return walk, all seemed even darker… until I looked up. Stars!

Stars and the planets grown huge, countless, and impossible to number, filled a clear sky as the crisp mountain air brought to sharp focus what must have been the Milky Way itself. Millions and billions of these points of light shined more brightly than I had ever witnessed before. And shooting stars, too! I stood, utterly spellbound, for at least a full two minutes. The meteors flashed across the night sky every thirty seconds with their streaking, long tails lingering.

"Wow! Justin! You need to get up and see this. Justin! Come outside and check out the stars tonight."

"What?" he groaned, sounding disturbed.

"You won't believe the sky tonight, so full of stars, brighter than you have ever seen them!" I answered.

"No! I don't want to. It's cold out there and I'm comfortable. I really don't care," he said with finality.

Day Six…

I arose at early dawn and was most surprised to find the guides already up and preparing a huge breakfast for the group. A cup of fresh-brewed coffee was ready and handed to me as I walked over to observe the morning meal being prepped. Then wandered over to the river to watch the sun begin creeping up into view, the rushing water reflecting the beams into a thousand dancing flashes as the river mist burned away. A second cup of joe was consumed while in conversation with some of the other rafting passengers, as we began congregating around the central activities of breakfast. There were several interesting customer profiles worthy of mention.

Our group originated from all over the country, and even included a family from London, England. The man was an investment banker, and was joined by his wife and two teen children on an "Across the Pond" summer holiday. There were two younger guys who were naval aviators stationed out of Connecticut, who flew P-3 anti-submarine patrol planes over the North Atlantic. One had brought along his fifteen-year-old sister from Montana. There was a retired couple from Kansas City who had brought along their thirteen-year-old grandson. A single, retired fellow working on his Bucket List planned on doing some fishing on this wilderness river, hoping to catch a Steelhead salmon, which travel from the ocean to spawning beds up river, near its source. Two professional career women from Detroit, also single and in their mid-thirties, were doing this long-planned adventure vacation as a mini-reunion, being old friends from college. All were quite friendly and sociable.

After attempting to rouse my son from his slumbers, I joined the elaborate display of a chow line. A long table was covered with fruits, yogurts, cold cereals, hot oatmeal, juices, milk, sausage and gravy, ham, bacon, eggs-to-order, omelets, cheeses, breads, muffins, and pancakes, with all the condiments laid out cafeteria style. Loading up a plate, I joined a group seated in the chairs set out from the night before and socialized while eating, comparing impressions from the first day while also speculating about what this new day had in store.

By eight-thirty, most of us were well fed and the lead guide, Matt, announced it was time to begin disassembling the camp. We pilgrims were instructed where to return the tents, cots, pads and personal baggage. Justin still had not risen from his slumbers, so it was a more agitating announcement I delivered to him as I began to pack up my own gear. He did finally get up and moving, and proved reasonably adept at dealing with his own responsibilities. We had finished our tent pack-up and delivered all gear just a few minutes ahead of the designated time.

Susan spied Justin as we were standing aside, observing four of the guides who were repacking the rafts. She walked up to ask if he had had anything to eat, interrupting her chores of last-minute cleanup and packing of the commissary area. Expressing major concern at his negative response, she, in a motherly but persistent tone, told him he must eat something. After he agreed to some pastries and juice, she quickly produced them, along with a bacon and egg sandwich. She apologized for it not being hot, but further cajoled him to consume it. Rolling his eyes in the classic "reprimanded teen" style, he did comply, which had me snickering. My own entreaties had failed to impact him that morning, so I was glad someone could make a difference for his dietary well-being. Susan was very special.

Our entire first-day transit of the river had been aboard one of the larger oar rafts, and Justin and I were now curious about how the paddle raft experience would compare. As people began forming around the raft or guide of choice, we declared that we'd like to try the faster and more vigorously participatory ride that morning. Natalie would be the steering guide, and the retired couple with the thirteen-year-old were also with us. I don't recall which major, place-named water obstacle was to be the "run" for that morning, but it was supposed to be a doozy.

And, oh indeed, it certainly was that.

We had been underway for about forty minutes and had run a couple of smaller rapids, just getting warmed up and used to the paddles, strokes, and pace. Natalie cheered us on and steered for the first of several big-waved waters as we paddled like mad to get the best speed. *Whoosh*, up and over we went, everyone splashed and soaked, and then on to the next. Hitting the second big wave was even better. We got airborne with an equal or even bigger splash and spray. The third came on very quickly, and onward we furiously paddled. We hit head-on, the front of the raft rising more than forty degrees up, and then back down we rolled in what felt a bit softer fashion than the last. The quieter water ahead gave little relieving pause as voices behind me cried, "Man overboard!"

As I turned around to view the scene, Natalie commanded us to "ship water," stalling the raft speed, and then she dove off the back. In less than a minute, she was swimming back with our thirteen-year-old lost passenger, and he was quickly hauled back on board. As the raft had crested over the last big wave, tipping downward, the rear had snapped upward, and he had been catapulted up and out like a bouncing ball. His foot had probably slipped out of the raft's safety strap, but nothing was said about it that I heard, then or later. It's part of the thrill factor.

Natalie swam over to my side of the raft, directly in front of my position. As she swung her leg up, attempting to hook it over the side, I grabbed her at the knee to assist her climb. The moving raft and water, slick skin from sun lotion, and my inadequate single-arm strength made it extremely difficult to pull her up. Leaning over as best I could without falling in myself, I reached higher on the thigh, but still without effect, the leverage still not enough. I then told her, as we struggled fruitlessly, that I would have to grab her butt— "Is that okay?" She said not to worry about it, so I did…a whole-cheek grab. But this rescue maneuver didn't work either. She was not that large a woman, but it was like there was an extra, invisible force pulling her back down, an undertow. After three more frustrating attempts to pull her up, she finally said, "Let me go." I did so immediately, and she was able to bob herself up enough to roll a leg over the tube again, and this time get into the raft by herself. I was very embarrassed. I did apologize profusely. She said, "Don't worry about it," and smiled nicely. Still…nothing stings like failure to aid a lady in distress.

Later, on the group lunch break, Justin complained that the paddle raft was too chilly for his thin blood, and preferred to switch back to one of the oar rafts for the afternoon runs. I wanted to get more photographs, so I agreed to the idea. We decided to rejoin Jake's raft, which had space available since the warmth of the day was now upon us, and others were interested in the paddle raft. The risks had been demonstrated as a real thrill deal.

The guides conducted a meeting away from the passengers before re-boarding the rafts, with Natalie and Susan appearing demonstrative while talking with Matt. I was later to learn that Susan had been training on an advanced rafting skills certification for the oar raft with Matt, and he was switching the roles and rafts of the two women for the afternoon before Susan's testing was completed. Both seemed less than pleased with the decision, and their glances in my direction gave pause. I wondered if I was at fault somehow.

Once underway, we took on the next sets of rapids, which were a softer experience in the larger boat. Jake identified points of interest like some old homestead structures and a couple of small, abandoned gold-prospecting remains. I couldn't help reflecting on how similar these little gold mines, literally small holes in the side of a rock hill, looked like open graves. There was nothing glamorous about them to my eye. Just dilapidated, mean little markers of a too-often futile past that may or may not have even yielded someone temporary subsistence, until all hope of finding undiscovered treasure died.

The Georgia Gold Rush was the second significant gold rush in the U.S. and would impact a greater area and thousands more people than the North Carolina gold fields, started in 1829. Several stories are told of the initial discovery the year before, but rumors of gold in the area had existed since early colonial times. These rumors, derived from the older tales told by Indians, explained that the small amounts of gold in their possession had come from the southern Appalachian Mountains. Other legends described that the French and Spanish had mined gold in northern Georgia from 1560 through 1690. The North Carolina find brought many fortune seekers to northern Georgia, believing the Indian rumors and legends as true. Once gold was reported there, thousands of people, infected with "Gold Fever," rushed to the area seeking to "get rich quick," with many encroaching on Indian treaty lands.

Concurrently, there was also great pressure on the Native American population from white settlers and plantation owners pushing westward and squatting on tribal lands. The state of Georgia even then had already passed legislation that would revoke the treaties signed by the Federal Government. The thousands of prospectors flooding the area were the last straw that enabled President Andrew Jackson to sponsor legislation to Congress called the Indian Removal Act of 1830. The following years witnessed the forced expulsion of all Indians not wishing to assimilate with white culture, and even many who did wish to assimilate, to lands west of the Mississippi River in Oklahoma.

Ultimately, there were over five hundred mines scattered among thirty-seven counties in the five states of the southern Appalachians. They would produce over 870,000 troy ounces of gold between 1828 and the mid-twentieth century.

The U.S. Mint set up a "branch mint" in the mining town of Dahlonega, Georgia, in 1838. Once the easy gold had been found, many of the miners moved west to participate in the California

Gold Rush of 1849 and the Colorado Gold Rush of 1859.

Many of the prospectors from California had also drifted up north and east into Nevada, Idaho, Wyoming, and Montana. Gold, silver, copper, and other valued metals were steadily discovered, and many disgruntled or disillusioned men from the Civil War deserted the carnage in the east to also attempt to strike it rich in the mountains. In 1864, four prospectors, known as the Georgians, found one of the early gold placers in Montana at Last Chance Gulch, which is the site of the state capital at Helena, Montana. Samuel Clemens, known as Mark Twain, was among those that made the journey to Nevada, and while prospecting brought him little success, writing about it led him to both fame and fortune. Within the three counties that our group was rafting through on the Middle Fork Salmon River, over thirty major mines were located, and of those outside the wilderness, several were still in operation.

Our raft was last in line when we turned through a bend in the river, all the others having moved ahead and out of sight momentarily. Once they were back in view, the reason for some overheard screams and shouting became clear. We beheld a water-gun battle underway among three of the craft about two hundred feet ahead. My mention that this might be a good time to pull over and observe the outcome was readily complied with by Jake. We had no water guns and were way too tempting as targets.

Just as we were settling back, watching the water-gunners reload their water weapons, a jet-blast of ice cold drenched my head, face, and entire torso from the right rear. What the...? When I turned to identify this unknown perpetrator, the gleefully smiling Natalie shot another long stream of frigid water from a high-capacity bazooka water gun. There was no escape. Her ambush was from one of the many tributary side streams and had taken some planning, and complicity too, no doubt. But Jake and Justin were also being hosed, so Jake commanded, "Justin! Board her raft and disarm this river renegade! Seize that weapon and bring it back!" as he steered our raft on collision course.

Upon contact, Justin and one of the other youngsters on our side of the battle leapt over to Natalie's raft, and a laughing, wrestling struggle ensued between the two and the other boat's occupants. My son successfully pirated Natalie's water gun and did return. Three casualties of the battle had fallen out of their raft and into the quiet water. Retaliation was swift now that our crew was able to defend itself with returned water sprays. A few minutes more and the skirmish was over, though I'm certain Natalie found her revenge on me very sweet. I had been duly punished for my failed water assist that morning, though it had been a worthy attempt… she did have a very fine posterior that any dirty old man could not fail to admire, so I was content to be playfully and indirectly reprimanded. The sin had been adjudicated venial and not mortal.

That evening we were treated to fire-grilled fresh salmon and haddock fish filets as entree' selection, along with an equally large variety of complimentary side dishes, salads, and desserts as previously. Our gathering after camp set-up was quite animated and even loud during the cocktail hour, and several more rafters participated in storytelling than the night before. The skies were clear and the air just a bit drier and warmer than the first evening, so the festivities ran even later. Even so, once the party dispersed for the night, most of the camp rested very quickly, comfortably, and soundly. My own tent had one more bit of excitement just after settling in.

"Oh! My! God!" a voice outside the tent slowly exclaimed.

"Oh…my…God!" echoed louder and more emphatically.

"Justin, are you all right?" I called out, now fully alert from the slumber I had been slipping into. Was he raising an alarm? The tent was dark, chilly, and the cold metal of the flashlight eluded my initial grasping from inside the sleeping bag. No other sounds, even from the group encampment, were audible.

"OH! MY! GOD!" my son for thrice repeated, shouting with awe and wonder.

After about another minute, he entered the tent and began stripping away his overcoat and boots in preparation to re-enter his own warm bedding for the night after this last rest room break.

"I *told* you last night had an awesome sky; well worth getting up for," I asserted as he settled in. "Did you see any meteors?"

"Yes! And the stars were so bright I could nearly touch them, it felt like. So many stars! Millions! It was like seeing the whole galaxy, the whole universe." His words were of reverence. *A Scout is Reverent.*

"They say there are billions. But what do they know?" I chuckled.

After a silence of mutual contemplation, Justin concluded, "Awesome…incredible."

Day Seven...

The start of the third day on the river mirrored the previous with another large breakfast followed by camp breakdown and repack for our continued wilderness voyage. Justin arose earlier this time, however, and we were ready to board an oar raft when Susan requested we join her paddle raft crew. I did agree, but my son declined, preferring the larger craft while the early chill was still in the morning air. He opted for Jake's craft again, and they lagged behind as our raft took the lead.

Our group moved downriver as an isolated flotilla, having a sense of privacy from other groups also on the river each day. Each rafting party was spaced about a mile apart, our only view of other people being when a switch of positions occurred at the breaks or evening campsites. The river runs of most of the commercial rafting parties were six-day affairs, which allowed extra time for fishing, hiking, or exploring some of the creek tributaries. There were some groups using rigidly constructed canoes and kayaks, but special licenses and skill certifications were required, extra fees, and the endurance of a two- or three-year waiting list for that kind of adventuring access. These private groups could traverse the distance in just four days, such as a Boy Scout Troop that canoed past our camp on this morning, leap-frogging ahead. The Forest Service and the commercial Guides worked carefully together to ensure that everyone derived maximum enjoyment and safety, alongside a sense of having the whole river as their own unique experience for as much of each day as possible.

Our adventure had begun in rugged hills of spruce and fir forests, with the Sawtooth Mountains as background. The terrain appeared more plateaued with increasing grass and shrub cover by the end of the second day and into the third. Then the mountains and canyons would appear with growing majesty as each mile passed by. On this day, we took a break at a natural hot spring. Both Justin and I indulged for about twenty minutes, immersing ourselves into a small pool of water of about four feet deep that was warmed by volcanic heat. Except for some mud, it was quite the relaxing experience.

There were also a few ancient Indian pictographs on the lower face of a large rock nearby that lent a primordial character to the entire area. No one volunteered what these pictographs meant or how old they were, and they struck me as very primitive and almost like graffiti. There are pictographs all over the United States, the oldest having been dated at around 1,100 B.C.E., but some are known to be as recent as the early twentieth century. It was mentioned within our group that many carved petroglyphs and rock art were also known to exist in some of the surrounding states, which could be dated considerably more ancient. The oldest in the Western Hemisphere, thought to be up to 12,000 years old, was found carved within a cave in Brazil and consisted of a stick figure with an oversized phallus, known as the "Horny Little Man."

At some point in the afternoon, another water fight erupted ahead, and our unarmed raft was again thoroughly soaked. It was there that my son and I were on opposite sides of the fray, and the Fates found us struggling over the same water weapon that had been tossed on shore. I hadn't wrestled with my boy since he was about five, and the physical advantage had clearly turned. I was most fortunate he relented before any serious test of wills might've spoiled the light fun that it was.

It was after this interesting interaction that I decided it best we stay together in future raft assignments and my paddle raft participation ended. Justin had no further interest in that physical exertion, either. I later learned that he had a more acute fear of the water than I ever realized, and felt less vulnerable with the softer ride of the larger rafts. The mischief of the younger crowd in the party, including some of the guides, would continue the rest of the day, but the old fogies (of which I began counting myself) made it clear that evening that not all were so thrilled with this particular diversionary game. The water guns were quietly stowed away and forgotten for the rest of the trip.

Day Eight...

On our fourth day on the river, the mountains and canyons grew huge. We were drawing near the lowest base point of Mount McGuire. Justin and I were both excited about nearing the place where it should become visible. Another photograph was the big discussion and objective for this final full day. But the first attraction, in addition to two more Class IV rapids, was stopping for lunch with extra time to check out a small but very beautiful waterfall just outside a large mountainside cave within a cirque. Several in our group took advantage of the cold shower it delivered, as the water fell some seventy-five feet from above. Others let out shouts to hear a double echo of their voices. Marco!... Polo!... was a favorite, along with, "Hey...You...Get-Off-Of-My-Cloud!" A bonus was added: as we departed the place, golden eagles could be observed perched near their nests on the cliffs across the river, and flying about in the sky high above.

The midafternoon stop was at a place called Big Creek Bridge, the single and only bridge over the Middle Fork of our transit. The bridge serves as the only connection of the trail system for hikers and those using horses, between the western and eastern halves of the wilderness that the river bisects south of the Main Salmon River. Several in the group decided to jump off the bridge into the river from a height of about fifteen feet. Too high and chilly for my blood—and Justin's. This was the first overcast day with diminished sun, and the darkened canyon walls and forest further dampened our enthusiasm for more cold and wet.

When initially planning the second road trip, I had investigated the possibility of hiking down the trail that this bridge is part of. We had considered climbing our mountain first, and then descending into this canyon via the eighteen-mile trail. We would then hook up with a rafting group and take the river out of the wilderness. Cool? No, no, no! Really, really, crazy nuts. A week-long conversation with our mountain outfitter and the rafting company (fortunately) proved my harebrained scheme unworkable. The terrain, as mentioned before, is some of the most rugged in the world, and my ambitions far outweighed our physical capabilities. The rafting company ultimately said they would still have to charge me full price...did I mention my penchant for bargain shopping? *A Scout is Thrifty.*

An interesting historical factoid occurred very near this spot in the wilderness that we had paused for at this break. About a quarter mile up Big Creek was where the 1879 Sheepeater Indian War had ended. The Sheepeater Indians were a subgroup tribe of the Shoshone, named after the mountain sheep that their diet consisted. Less than five hundred people were directly involved in the affair, but it lasted almost six months and covered a crisscrossing trail of pursuit exceeding twelve hundred miles of this wilderness area. After months of frustrations and inconclusive small engagements, one of the fugitive chiefs, named War Jack, finally walked into the pursuing U.S. Army's camp, located as described above. He said that he was "tired of running and fighting." The remaining fifty-one Indian men, women, and children fugitives surrendered with him.

Even the natives here get tired out by the terrain.

Our group stayed about an hour at the bridge and then shoved off for the final leg before arrival at our next campsite, and a view of our Mount McGuire from its western base was now at hand. My planned photo-op was pretty much a bust, however. At the point in the river we were located when bypassing it, the solid-rock-faced canyon walls exceeded four hundred feet and were very near vertical in most cases. Only sky could be observed beyond the tops of the canyon walls. Any sense of the peak over one mile above was not discernible from the river. There was a small sign posted on the rock wall designating Mount McGuire (that did suddenly appear), but our raft was moving so fast that I couldn't get a picture before we flashed by. Rafts have very poor brakes in fast water.

The final campsite was the smallest and most tightly-packed of the journey, a natural amphitheater with sheer rock walls, hundreds of feet high on three sides. There were a few small scrub brush trees, just enough to hide the portable-commode restroom off in the corner. Though we were stopping at our usual time of the evening, the clouds and the canyon walls gave a darker and slightly gloomy atmosphere to the place. It matched the mood of our rafting family, foreseeing that our adventure together would be ending the next day. We were at the doorstep of "Impassible Canyon," and its name left nothing to the imagination. It was a lively dinner hour, but a muted campfire gathering afterward, as most folks turned in early, well used up for the day.

Day Nine…

The last morning on the river followed the routines of the prior three, with a big breakfast, camp breakdown, and all-a-board the rafts by about ten o'clock. The river was running fast and deep as we descended through the canyon on rough water that had multiple waves rippling across the surface. There was less white water, but the raft moved with great speed over plenty of bumps and rolls as we navigated dead center of the current. The dark granite canyon walls rose straight up from each side of the river's edge, with no shore-line breaks, thus the one-way, nonstop ride was very similar to a tunnel at times. About an hour later, the Main Salmon River opened into view with the bright light of midday.

At the confluence of the Main Salmon and Middle Fork, the largest rapids and waves of the entire trip were encountered. The splash, spray, rolling, and paddling up and over large four- to five-foot-high whitecaps served as our grand finale, uninterrupted by calm waters until the last quarter-mile. Suddenly, we were at journey's end, and we made landfall within about seven minutes after that final magnificent thrill.

There was quite a large congregation of people from two preceding rafting groups already present at Cache Bar, our group's river takeout point. A flurry of activities were conducted by the guides, forest rangers, and vehicle transportation people as we thrill pilgrims disembarked the rafts and made our way to an awaiting bus for transit back to town. In about thirty minutes, the baggage, supplies, equipment, and rafts themselves had been repacked and loaded up for the return to civilization. The bus traced a narrow gravel road upstream along the river to the namesake town of Salmon. Matthew announced an invitation from the River Guide Team for one last evening of farewell at their favorite pizza pub in town. We pilgrims were all very enthused, and most of us accepted the invite.

Justin and I easily recovered my Ford Ranger pickup truck at one of the Salmon motel parking lots, which the rafting company had helped arrange to be conveyed from Stanley. We then proceeded to our favorite coffee shop for lunch and to kill part of the ninety minutes before early motel check-in time. Since I can't remember the cuisine we indulged, it was probably hamburgers and fries, that not having been a menu item the previous five days. Once checked into our rooms, we showered and napped off some of the accumulated fatigue of our first whitewater river rafting adventure. And sleep we did, for about two hours, and then found ourselves walking in late to our last rendezvous with the group, the party already well underway.

These festivities were another high point of the rafting trip. The guides circulated about the group, ensuring each person was well satisfied, and entertained with chat and stories amongst pizza, beer, and soft drinks. They thanked each participant on behalf of the rafting company as well as personally. Of course, this was also the time where we customers could return our own thanks and tip the squad for their tireless and devoted services. Our river guides had been "on-the-job" for at least seventeen to eighteen hours each day of the journey and relentlessly committed to the notion that every customer felt this to be an unforgettable vacation experience. Our guide crew exceeded all expectations.

Our own reciprocated thanks to Natalie, Matthew, Jake, Susan, George, and Josh also disclosed that my son and I would be starting our expedition to climb our mountain the following day. I promised to give each of them their own piece of Mount McGuire from the summit, since it looked as though we might be able to meet once again in one week's time. The guides were all excited about that, since it would give them an extra story to tell while rafting by the mountain, or at evening campfires for the balance of the season. Our party continued for a couple of hours and photos were taken and liberally shared. The comradery we enjoyed with each other provided a few last sweet moments to be savored in the years to follow.

With one last round of farewells, we took our leave at dark and returned to the motel for rest. We would need it. Phase two of our expedition would commence the next day: we would behold the true object of this Road Trip endeavor, and perhaps accept the challenge of its invitation for conquest – Mount McGuire.

CHAPTER
ELEVEN

Day Ten…

"Woke up … fell out of bed … dragged a comb across my head…
Found my way downstairs, and drank a cup… and looking up, I
noticed I was late…
Found my coat … and grabbed my hat… Made the bus, in
seconds flat…
Found my way upstairs, and had a smoke … and somebody
spoke, and I went into a dream…"
"A Day in The Life," Lennon/McCartney, 1967

After re-acquaintance with civilized sleep accommodations of the motel beds and indoor plumbing, Justin and I arose with the sun well up in the sky. The personal ritual of orientating my day had been comfortably transferred to the favorite local coffee shop, with indulgence in a leisurely breakfast. Conversation focused on the next phase and what duties were required before our departure back into the wilderness.

The most immediate task of calling the outfitter company, to confirm our mountain horse transport, had been completed the prior day upon arrival at the motel. I had been in regular long-distance telephone communication with them since the preceding December, and they had been most helpful with fine-tuning our objectives and goals. We had encountered the owner the year before, he being the civilian with the two forest rangers we had met on first arrival at the Crags Trailhead on Road Trip One. He was quite friendly over the telephone and had shared a couple of stories of great interest that guided some of our decisions. One fact shared was that a few folks climbed Mount McGuire every year and it would be no problem if we chose to do a climb.

The plan was to drive to the outfitter's camp at the Crags Trailhead that evening and spend the night there. The next morning, a guide would then assist our traversing a distance by horseback, with our gear on packhorse, to a lake within an hour hike of the mountain itself. Four days later, the guide would return to pick us and our gear up, lead us via horseback to the trailhead camp, from where we would proceed back down into town before nightfall. A simple plan, and after the last experience, money well spent to ensure success.

We needed to replenish clean laundry after our nine days of nonstop travel and fun. The drop-off service laundromat discovered the prior year proved once again a perfect solution and promised completion within four hours. Though the motel check-out was smooth enough, news of the establishment's policy on reservations and late check-ins added an unforeseen rigidity to our timeline. If we failed to arrive by eight o'clock in the evening for check-in, and if overbooking existed, which was frequent during the summer season, our room could be given away, the reservation lost, and the office would also close at that hour.

Proceeding on to a sporting goods store, we bought fishing licenses, bait, and a couple of other useful camping items. The owner of the shop was most helpful in the bait selections that he reported were very successful with attracting the fish in the mountain lakes of that area. We also purchased lures advertised to catch the "really big ones" that were known to be plentiful in the area as well.

From there we moved down the block to the local grocery store, intent on stocking up on foods for the planned six days of camping. A portion of our meals would be canned or freeze dried, but we also wanted fresh eggs, bacon, cheese, milk, sandwich meats, bread, and fresh fruits. The trick would be to pack them according to the "survivability of transit" rule.

Our initial departure time had been projected for about two o'clock in the afternoon, so after lunch we collected the clean laundry, gassed up the Ranger, and were successfully on our way very close to schedule. Though the sixty-mile distance had taken us about four hours and fifteen minutes to traverse on Road Trip One, with our new and better-equipped vehicle we were tracking a time closer to a three-hour timeline.

Up the first mountainside switchback we cruised, the previous year's road construction now complete. Down into the valley of Panther Creek's scenic wonder we continued to the town of Cobalt (still population: one). The trout-fishing visitor's section was more populous. Numerous vehicles, tent-campers, and RVs stretched across the field between the road and creek bank. Since the main building near the road had a few vehicles parked by the door, we decided to stop in and see if we could acquire a fresh bag of ice, an overlooked purchase before we had left Salmon.

On entering the dark wood-framed structure, our eyes slowly adjusted to the dim interior, which was a big contrast with the bright sunny day outside. There were a couple of men sitting at a bar in this front room, so we ambled over to it looking for who might be able to help us. Soon, a fellow entered the area from a connected meeting room, and smiled as he asked, "What can I do for you?"

"We were hoping to buy some ice," I answered. "Do you have any you can spare?"

"Yeah, I can sell you some for three bucks. Bring in your cooler and I'll load you up."

Justin was already moving to the door to bring in the cooler, so I continued speaking with the man, who had moved behind the bar near his ice machine. "You all look pretty full up with fisherman today. How long do folks usually stay for their trout fishing here?"

"Oh, it varies. Some just show up for an overnight, and others stay all season until September. On the week-ends we can have two-hundred people, sometimes."

"Do you have a brochure I can take with me for future reference, so I can call ahead?" I asked with a laugh.

Just then my son returned with the cooler, and as the barman began filing it, he said, "We don't have a telephone here. It's part of our Shtick. There is a business card you can have at the end of the bar, there," pointing to the location.

I walked over to where a stack of the cards lay, and took one. It was a card folded double, the front saying, Panther Creek Fishing Lodge. Opening the fold, the left panel read: Best Fly Fishing Resort in the West. No Phone. No Solicitors. No Troubles. Address: The Middle of Nowhere, Idaho. A small sketch road map filled the second panel.

With another laugh I said, "I guess I'll just have to take my chances next time."

"Yes, you will, but most people win around here," he said with a wink. "That'll be just two dollars, sir, 'cause this cooler is small. When you come back down from the mountain, stop in for a two-for-one beer special."

"I think we just might do that in about a week. Thank you very much for your kind assistance."

"Good luck!" the barman said with a wave, as we exited the building into the bright sunshine.

Continuing up this creek-side road, we soon found the turn-off to our destination. There the route required marked reduction in speed due to the still-present mega-ruts, holes, and narrower track. Thus, at the next mountain road intersection where a large graveled area was located, Justin and I agreed to stop in order to water the roadside shrubs. The elapsed time since departure was at the ninety-minute mark.

Within five minutes we were continuing, gunning the four-wheel drive back up the mountain track. The road was pretty good there, given the overall complexion of this passageway, so it was surprise indeed when I could sense the Ranger's tires pulling from the path being steered. After about the third time I noticed this new quirk, I pulled over to look at renewed tire suspicions.

Son. Of. A. Beech (tree)*!* Road Demons!

The front right tire was already half flat. *Mother Fletcher*!

The uphill grade we were traversing was also tilted about fifteen degrees and was quite narrow; no turning around was possible, so a tire change required continuing upward and finding a flatter, wider area. Though these mountain roads were sparsely traveled, there had been other traffic coming down the mountain that had right-of-way. And there was also no doubt someone could have been behind us. This city boy wanted no part in causing a traffic jam in the wilderness. So onward we climbed for half-a-mile before the proper terrain was reached.

I had never changed a truck tire before, and I was more than just displeased that my first lesson would occur here. The first task was to find the jack, but the driver's manual easily located it for me, hidden away behind a panel within the cab. This terrain was better than before, but still far from perfect. The vehicle did slip off the jack while loosening the lug-nuts, but no damage was done. I did better securing the jack on my second attempt. Justin helped where he could, but was as inexperienced as I with proper methodology. After furious activity, many new cussing combinations, and two other vehicles passing us by with a wave and an audible, "Sorry about your luck," the tire was successfully changed. The procedure and my slow learning curve had eaten about an extra hour.

We pulled into the outfitter's wilderness camp as the clock was ticking near seven, and were heartily greeted by the cowboy staff awaiting us. They showed us to accommodations that were quite nice. Our shelter was a modified eight-man wall tent raised on a wooden deck platform, with four upraised wooden bed pedestals and a wood-burning stove.

The leader of the camp was the owner's manager of operations and was acquainted with our contracted needs. He took the time to settle monetary accounts while reviewing our usage of two riding horses and two pack horses, but quoted a price less than I'd remembered discussing. We were invited to share their cowboy stew dinner, but I declined, having set my heart on the steaks Justin and I were now most eager to reward ourselves with after our latest transportation ordeal. He also immediately offered to have the damaged tire repaired while we were away on our adventure, and with my thanks for this service, we completed transfer of the tire to his possession. On that note he took his leave, wishing us good luck and a good time.

Justin and I then set ourselves to unpacking the gear from the vehicle and the dinner prep chores. Soon we were eating a righteous meal of chargrilled steak, potatoes, and baked beans, topped off with a glass of merlot that enhanced all the flavors. But this respite was not followed by continued relaxation. After clean-up, we spent the next two hours repacking our gear, equipment, foods, and supplies for what was to come in the next five days. We focused on leaving nonessentials, but were careful to include several new comfort items: a portable shower, folding camp chairs, and the required extra soft drinks and wine. What kind of fun is it to climb a mountain if you can't enjoy a fine glass of Cabernet at the top? The time was near midnight before we turned-in to our beds, the chill of the damp evening mountain air having transformed our breath to frosty.

Day Eleven...

The livestock corralled at the camp began stirring at first light, adding to the discomfort of the wood pedestal beneath my back, and a full bladder. On return from the outhouse, the resident cowboys could also be heard beginning their own constitutionals, so I encouraged Justin to also rise. He did so by the time I was heating water for my second cup of instant coffee with my newly purchased gas cooking burner, and it was about then that one of the cowboys came over to check in and offer us some of their breakfast.

It was a basic affair of cold cereals, milk, hot oatmeal, some fire-fried sausage, and bread—a good start. While eating, our two cowboys instructed to bring what we planned to pack with us to the corral in about thirty minutes. We returned to the tent, hauled what was ready, and packed the remnants back in the truck. Our guides had their own chores to complete as well, and it was another, extra half hour before they started packing the horses.

Watching the packing was a bit of a show. All seemed nearly complete as our cowboys easily filled two large double-pouch saddlebags with all our baggage. Suddenly, one of the fully loaded packhorses started a fit of bucking, displeased by the load it was saddled with. Before our eyes, the precious gear that wasn't fully secured began flying high into the air and crashing to the ground, including our two lawn chairs and the ice cooler with its contents. Miraculously, there was no damage done except to three of the ten eggs that I had especially packed—and we lost most of our ice, of course! But after a quick repack, Robert, the lead guide, announced it was time to mount up, and away we rode down the trail into the forested wilderness.

Justin had reported to me that his horse-riding experience consisted of just two short rides at a summer camp in his earlier youth. My own experience consisted of little more. We were tenderfeet by all measures, so after the initial slow, startup walk of these beasts of burden, as their pace increased, so did our discomfort. As long as the horse stayed at a walk on the rising ground, the ride *did* beat hiking. But on level ground, my horse tended to break into a trot to catch up with the leader. This would bang my crotch blue unless I stood in the stirrups, a relief I quickly learned and embraced. When we started downhill, all my muscles in contact with the saddle wore very tender right quick. Fortunately, Robert called for a foot-walking interval during most of the downhill trail portions to rest the animals.

Robert fit well the iconic image of the American western cowboy of the nineteenth century. He was twenty years of age, just shy of six feet tall, slender yet well-conditioned, and had a youthful face with eyes that exuded certainty of purpose and deep experience. He was not chatty, restricting his comments to the obvious requirements of safe passage for the most part, only adding details that made clear his love of this wilderness and his satisfaction with living and working in it. He was knowledgeable about and devoted to the animals we were riding, sharing the histories and riding tendencies of each horse in our group, as well as basic coaching for easy control and care.

At our first break, we had just passed through the first group of rock towers near the Cathedral Rock landmark where I had experienced such odd mental sensations and felt a physical chill the year before. The physical chill sensation once again came upon me this transit, and at the break I shared this with our group while asking if they too felt anything odd.

The cowboys denied having any, and Justin, taking his cue from them, remained silent. Okay, fine! I decided to settle for the notion that my imagination was

The Towers

mischievous and took a much-enjoyed cigarette break. It was easy to just admire the surrounding forested mountains, dramatic rock formations and towers, valleys, bright sun, and blue skies while snapping a few photos. Our pause lasted about ten minutes, and then it was "back in the saddle again."

We had leisurely ridden only fifty to one hundred meters farther along the top of the ridge. I was casually gazing about, struck by the majesty of the landscape. Suddenly, to my right something stood out in acutely sharp contrast to all the ruggedly natural topographic beauty, something seemingly so out of place that I halted my horse abruptly for a more studied look. "What the hell is that?" I shouted in complete wonder.

The Sentinel

We all congregated at my object of discovery and consternation.

"What is a statue doing way out here?" I questioned as we gazed upon a large granite structure some eight meters away from our position. The object appeared to be at least five to ten meters tall and carved into what looked like a bust of an Indian chief. Thoughts of the ancient Aztec or Mayans came to my mind.

"It's just a rock." Robert spoke authoritatively.

With very conventional elucidation Robert continued, "This wilderness area is full of odd and interesting geological rock structures, but they're still just rocks. It's part of why it's great out here. So, now we need to move along because we are a little behind schedule."

Off he and the group headed. But I was not completely convinced and wanted evidence. I held back a few extra moments, long enough to snap photographs of this and yet another strange rock. The second, even larger "rock" looked like the bust of a lion, or even some strange alien collage of beasts and humanoids. Very strange, and kinda creepy.

My new-found standing-while-trotting lesson helped me catch up quickly to the group.

We continued on this familiar section of trail for less than a mile and then split off on a second trail that took us downward. This new trail descended gradually but steadily about six hundred feet, where at the next trail intersection a new path would lead back up another mountainous ridge. As we made our way downward, several hiking and saddle horse pairs and groups were passed hiking upward. One group was using two llamas as their baggage carriers. My count was perhaps twenty people in all. The wilderness seemed more populated than last year.

The daytime sun was bright and the temperature warmer. By the time we had climbed up to and arrived at Birdbill/Gentian Lakes, we had emptied both water flasks brought for the journey. It had been a beautiful and scenic ride, but Justin and I were painfully saddle sore and could hardly tolerate riding horseback another meter. We were also too depleted to do much more than watch in dumb silence as the cowboys unloaded our gear to the ground.

Scouting and finding a nice tent site about fifty meters from the drop off, we began moving our gear while the cowboys ate their lunch. Before we were finished, Robert met us to confirm our pickup time in four days. Then he and his assistant mounted up and rode away. Return to the trailhead camp with our horses in tow needed to occur before sundown, and it was past two o'clock in the afternoon already. Their round trip and camp chores to follow qualified as a long work day in anyone's book.

Justin and I set to raising our tent, arranging our bedding, stowing supplies and equipment, and then finally putting together and eating our own lunch. Next was to replenish our water supply from a handy stream flowing between the two lakes that our campsite was located near. One of the lessons learned from the previous year was to secure our own small, light-weight water purifier. It worked like a charm.

After completion of these tasks, I realized that our camp chairs were missing. Somehow these two items, that the last years' experience had proven to us a much-missed convenience for extended camping, had not made the packhorse transit. Disappointment number one was followed quickly by frustration number one: my attempt to start a campfire.

Under less tiring circumstances, I would not have made the error that occurred. In haste to accomplish the task, I tried shortcutting the tried and true method. I substituted a bit of cardboard paper, which at that altitude and higher, tends to smolder without flame and ultimately smother. It did so repeatedly over the next ten minutes of failed attempts. *Aaahhhckt!* Too tired to rant for long, I joined Justin in the tent to rest and reboot mind and body. The proper altitude acclimation had not been completed, and the horseback riding would be the only shortcut the mountain gods would allow that day.

My reboot consisted of quickly passing out into a two-hour nap. It was after five o'clock in the evening before Justin and I stirred, but we were refreshed from the adventurous ordeals of the day. The second attempt at kindling a campfire proved remarkably successful once using all natural ingredients, so our supper prep commenced once the fire blazed up bright, hot, and strong. We cooked up some canned beef stew with extra vegetables and ground beef. All was prepared, eaten, cleaned up, and stowed away before nightfall was upon us. Provision was made for animal-proofing our edibles outside the tent, and we relaxed for about an hour playing some cards. By full dark, our lights went out. It was still chilly but noticeably warmer this second night up in these mountains.

Justin had a better-cushioned ground pad, the new gas lamp heated the tent to a more tolerable temperature, there was a forest service pit-toilet within easy distance, and water was in substantial supply. All in all, we were prepared with more comforts in general. The coffee and cigarettes were available in small but useful quantity such that my tension tantrums had only occurred during the second tire episode and my failure to produce fire earlier. Paranoia of the dark had subsided because another couple of campers some hundred meters away had brought a dog, who howled half the night making himself the perfect bear or big cat bait. We slept well.

Day Twelve...

My travel clock read just before six o'clock in the morning when I rose for this day, and the chill air brought added urgency to rekindling the fire that served us so well the evening before. There were still a few live coals that had survived the water dousing the previous night, so a nice blaze was accomplished quickly. It was accompanied by a mind-clearing coffee and a tobacco treat. The dawn indicated another sun-filled day. Sounds soon confirmed that the other campsite was beginning their own morning, so I used this as justification to serve Justin notice that it was time for him to end his slumbers and also arise.

By 7:30 A.M. Justin joined me, and though hidden by the surrounding mountains, the sun was well up and the day bright and beautiful. Our campsite was located in a small, bowl-shaped valley containing the twin alpine lakes known as Gentian and Birdbill. Our campsite was closest to Gentian Lake, surrounded by forested mountains, large ridges of granite rock, and spires. Up close was a view of Fishfin Ridge, where our previous year's backpacking hike had met an exhausted end two miles short of this place.

We set to preparing a hearty, hot breakfast of scrambled eggs, bacon, bread, cheese, fresh fruit, and milk. While eating and cleaning up, we talked about exploring the way to our Namesake Mountain to judge up close if it was within our climbing means, and take pictures. I'd read a few print descriptions of this locale, but none came close to what a photograph would reveal, even a thousand words falling all too short.

Nature called me shortly after the meal, so opportunity to inspect the outhouse on the other side of the lake was acted upon. Daily constitutionals completed, I then decided to look in on our neighboring campers and their dog during my return walk back. Their camp was sited on Birdbill Lake, and as I approached, I hailed a fellow stooped over a campfire, obviously working on breakfast. The dog, an eighty-pound Labrador Retriever, came over to greet me with a wagging tail. The man looked up with a smile, and a woman lying on her side, looked out from their tent.

I introduced myself as their neighbor across the water and told where I was from and what my son and I were up to. They reciprocated, informing that they had hiked in from the Crags trailhead via the path Justin and I had attempted the year before. They had chosen to attempt the Beaver Slide, and the woman had suffered injury on a rock hidden by snow, that had severely bruised her lower back and posterior. This explained her restful position. She said they would likely return to town tomorrow after she rested her back for the day. I expressed my condolences, wished them a safe return, and took my leave.

Upon my return to our campsite to complete daily hygiene requirements, I discovered Justin back in bed. Encouragement for him to also use the public facility was met with a growl, but he did comply. While he was thus engaged, I began prepping lunches, KP chores, securing the campsite, and assembling the camera, water, first-aid kit, rope, and other implements I felt might be useful for our planned explorations. When Justin returned, he helped with what he could, and we then prepped ourselves for the hike.

By about 10:15 A.M. we were ready and set off onto the forested ridge switchback trail that the map indicated would take us to the object of this five-hundred-day obsession. The climb was about two hundred feet to the top of what the hiking trail guide descriptions called a "Saddle Ridge," that connected the geological structures forming Aggipah Mountain to the south and Mount McGuire to the north. Within the valley were two more alpine lakes, the first coming into view just past the saddle summit. It was called Airplane Lake, with water the darkest blue I had ever beheld. It was only a few more steps down the path that Ship Island Lake also came into view, terraced lower and farther out in the valley. A small copse of lodge-pole pine trees were growing from an island of rock in the center of its equally blue water. This was absolutely the most incredible and enchanting view of landscape my son and I had ever seen in our lives.

Mt. McGuire

The tree cover still obscured full view of the mountains themselves, but as we progressed down the trail, first Aggipah and then Mount McGuire did reveal their full majesty. Justin and I had discussed over the previous year that the gradual rise of the pyramidal spine of our mountain, discernible from the photograph taken the previous year, might offer our best chance of scaling the edifice. As we beheld in much closer personal proximity the complete mountain, the possibility transformed into a real probability, and our pace quickened toward this new challenge. I had to force the issue of slowing down in order to take the first of several pictures of this valley and our mountain. Each new vantage point offered a new composition of emerald forest, dark blue waters, jagged spires of gray granite, huge boulders, snow-covered mountains, clouds on blue sky, and alpine flowers in full bloom.

Using the map as our guide, we reached what appeared to be the closest point of the trail from which a departure from, would be the shortest distance to the mountain peak. Striking out from there, we walked on a rising slope through the trees. Within about fifteen minutes an eroded embankment, or shelf, of about six feet in height appeared. It looked scalable. With little trouble, we hoisted ourselves up, taking advantage of scrub-brush handholds, and found that the tree line ended there. A gradually ascending open plateau covered with rock and boulders was the new topography. A clear avenue to the rocky mountain spine seemed obvious, so we continued our forward movement, picking our way through the rock and boulder field.

The sky had become overcast while we made our way across this landscape, but the day's temperature had also risen enough that we stripped off our coats and tied them around our waists. After about an hour we had covered about half a mile to the objective and begun a true rock climb, on all fours, along the mountain spine. This was not quick movement; in fact, after about another hour, we were still not within sight of the peak. The rocks and boulders on the mountain had grown monstrously huge, many as large as automobiles.

We stopped at a rock tower that presented itself as a great shaded lunch-break spot. The sun's solar rays were still burning through, and another douse of sunscreen was also called for. After consuming some much-needed food and water, I took a few photos of the area from this perspective.

The tower struck me as very odd on closer inspection. It strongly resembled a large cairn, approximately twenty to twenty-five feet in height. The boulder-sized granite rocks were huge, most weighing a ton and more, and they appeared stacked to neatly fit together. With such symmetry and tight lines, one might've imagined them being deliberately fashioned, strongly resembling a rougher version of the large limestone blocks often used for church cathedrals and government buildings. Gazing back down the mountain spine of jumbled boulders, at least two other distinct stacks of large rocks seemed to be visible. Impossible! Who could have done such a thing, and how? *Why*?

This rock structure appears to be diliberately stacked. An ancient Cairn?

After the break, we once more set out to continue the rocky climb. But after about twenty minutes, the size of the boulders began to totally obstruct our path unless we climbed down from the spine significantly. After looping downward nearly a hundred feet or so, shifting our angle of ascent, and climbing back up, the incline steepened considerably, and with additional boulder obstruction. It was clear to me that we were getting in over our heads in both skill and experience.

The summit was visible, and Justin was more than exasperated when I called a halt to our climb. He was pumped with adrenalin and psyched to continue to the top. We debated his point of, "Being so close, the time is now!"

His youth and enthusiasm had charged him up with rare passion. I was most concerned with the increasing difficulty of this particular path and the lateness of the day. Additional fears were that even if we did make it to the top, it would take just as much time getting down as it had taken to make the ascent. We could be caught far out of camp after dark. With no flashlight packed for the day-hike, the trail very rugged, and with our cross-country path being more than a little treacherous, I was not as confident.

It was my calculation that the climb would take another hour or even ninety minutes to reach the summit, but possibly more. It was three o'clock in the afternoon. Since we'd consumed half the water already, I asked, "Why push our luck?" Pointing up to a darkening, overcast sky, I continued, "So what if it starts to rain? Tomorrow will be easier now that we know the lay of the land better. We have two more days!" Lightning storms in the mountains can be deadly.

Justin relented. With a silent sigh of relief on my part, and a snort of disgust from my son, back down we climbed. A short drizzling rain did in fact accompany us during the hike back on the forest trail. We arrived at the campsite just after seven o'clock that evening, thirsty and hungry.

After a ten-minute collapse, we rekindled the campfire and prepped an easy "just-boil-water" rice & chicken dinner, supplemented with crackers and cheese, some wine, and two Advil. It was dark by the time cleanup was complete, and renewed energies had my son and I sitting by the fire, reviewing the climb. The awesome beauty of our discoveries had us excitedly planning how to take on the mountain with full force on the morrow. But shortly, raindrops again began to fall. We retired to the tent and our beds entirely well spent, yet inspired by our accomplishments and looking forward to the next day.

Fishfin Ridge in the far center, the forest covered Saddle, the geologic bowl behind the Saddle is our campsite.

CHAPTER
TWELVE

July 22, 1997, Day Thirteen…

Nutrition and sanitation are two major areas of concern that, if not addressed with vigilance, can make for a very miserable time, particularly during extended camping out in the wilds. Hand sanitizer and strong bleach detergent were mandatory pack and use items. We were fortunate to have a provided pit toilet shelter nearby at this location, though the facility was still quite crude. It also had a very large mosquito and biting fly population within. An effective bug repellant was vital, and the most effective was a product named "100% Deet." We had packed plenty and used it liberally, with good results concerning insect bites, but the protection had several fine-print warnings about side effects.

The side effects mentioned included skin rash, mucous membrane irritation, ocular irritation, dizziness, disorientation, difficulty concentrating, lethargy, auditory hallucination, severe agitation, grandiose delusion, belligerence, and aggressiveness. It was strongly recommended to wash all treated skin daily before sleeping. But the stuff did work great, and given the insect populations near the lakes, streams, and in any tree-cover whatsoever at this time of the year, we considered the risk/reward a good trade-off. The only side effect we had noticeably suffered had been the mucous membrane irritation, but the high-altitude triggered sinus congestion anyway, and masked that symptom, and which usually cleared up once one just blew his nose.

Given the physical workout of this adventure, I had been very conscious of our menu containing multiple sources of protein. That morning, it was bacon and eggs fried over-easy, just like Mom would cook them when I was a kid. We also consumed bread, cheese, bananas, instant Tang, and milk that would fortify our bodies for this day of pushing to the top. Lunch would consist of turkey and cheese sandwiches, apples, and granola bars to boost our energy.

The sun was well up before we were moving along with preparations on this morning, and Justin seemed to be considerably slower than I'd expected. He seemed oblivious of the morning tasks, and I no doubt "dogged" him with complaint that did little to create teamwork. It was nearly eleven o'clock before we were ready, once again starting later, but we set out more confidently and more clear about our objective. The time could be made up since it would not be expended with as many of the photographic indulgences. At the top of the Saddle Ridge we opted for a break, and while we rested, along came another hiker who decided on a short break of his own.

His name was Thomas, and he hailed from Boise, Idaho. He was about my own age and disclosed he was an avid outdoorsman who was planning to climb Mount McGuire that day. Tom said that his first attempt had failed when he was much younger, and for one reason or another, it had taken him twenty years to get back for another try. On sharing our own intention to also climb the mountain, he granted our request to accompany him, this stroke of luck appearing too good to be true. He shared that he had scaled several mountains over the years, and he looked the part both physically and in bearing. Tom was the perfect picture of a two-hundred-pound athlete with thick-muscled legs, a broad chest, and golden, tanned skin. He promised to take an easy pace while in the lead, but warned that we would have to do our best to keep up with him or he would have to leave us behind.

Leading on, he was good to his word and we kept up well enough with him on the path. He chose to continue past where Justin and I had broken away from the trail the previous day, but found his own break-away point not much farther down into the valley. The approach through the trees was noticeably steeper, but we were lined up with a straighter path to the peak.

When deciding to take our lunch, we were just beyond the tree line and had completed traversing the rock-strewn plateau. While eating, Tom inquired as to how a couple of Hoosiers had found themselves in this area, noting that even most people from Idaho had little knowledge of its existence. It was then that I revealed our last name and that it only made sense to take your son to climb a mountain with his name on it. Tom most likely put aside any notion of ditching us at that point, even though it was clear we were a real drag on his climb. He transformed himself into our good shepherd.

Setting out after about twenty-five minutes of rest, we soon were climbing over and between boulders and rocks on all fours. Tom led the way ever closer to the mountain spine, and then we began to move laterally just below the spine's edge. Tom had advanced a good twenty or thirty meters ahead when I called out to Justin that I needed an emergency break, my bowels suddenly demanding relief for the second time this day. Justin returned with the back-pack long enough to hand over the small quantity of emergency

Another Sentinel?

toilet paper I had included in our hike prep, and behind a large rock the very urgent business was dealt with. In about seven minutes, this bodily function and mental sacrilege was completed, and we hurriedly moved on to where Tom had stopped. The first and only potential obstruction to the climb lay before him, and he waited patiently as we neared his position. It was his intention to demonstrate for us a simple maneuver to overcome it.

A nakedly smooth, seven-foot-wide sheet of exposed mountain granite slanting at a forty-five-degree angle had to be crossed to continue this path of ascent. The granite sheet continued at least twenty-five meters down the mountainside to dirty rock debris that continued at similar angle another eight hundred feet or more. One slip and it would be a very long and rough tumbling descent. One slip and it would hurt…a lot.

Tom quickly explained how a solid, single step with full weight would work well on the surface. He then took one large step and was on the other side with a second step, his boot having held firm. It looked so easy—except for one thing. My legs were not as long as his, and it was clear to me that I would require a second step on the angled granite to accomplish the crossing, a total of three steps. When I mentioned that the distance was too far for us to copy-cat, Justin said, "No, it's not, see?" He duplicated the two-step maneuver with ease and stood safely on the other side, smiling back at me.

They both attempted to cajole and encourage me for a couple of minutes to go for it. But my calculation of distance and steps was not proven differently. I declined, stating that my son and I would figure something out. In my mind's eye, all I could see was my boot slipping on my extra step and the plunge that would ensue. Tom decided to move on, and Justin stared at me with a lost look. The summit was only another sixty meters or so higher. As Tom moved on, Justin continued pleading with me to make the attempt, but doubt grew stronger, as did a powerful sense in both of us that a lifetime opportunity might be slipping away.

Finally, a solution came to me.

"Get some of the rope out of the hiking pack, Justin, and throw me one end of it. I just need that little extra support for the second step I have to take."

Emotions were high, and as Justin began rummaging through the pack, we heard Tom hooting and shrieking celebration from a distance. He declared that he'd made it and called for us to come on up.

"It's easy!" he shouted.

Justin was having difficulties with my requested task. For what felt like many minutes, it was a vision of dawdling futility to watch him. As a bit of wind came up, I looked down the mountain and saw a ghostly dust cloud pass by below. I suddenly felt precarious and absolutely helpless. A huge and all-consuming fear and panic from a vertigo attack was sweeping over me.

"Dammit, Justin, hurry up! It's bad for me here, and I'm 'losing my shit!'" I yelled.

My son desperately pulled out all three ropes hopelessly tangled in a glob that had resisted any single one to pull free. Something else fell out of the pack and tumbled down the granite sheet as he did so.

"What was that? Justin, what just now fell out of the pack?" I shouted.

"The camera," he answered, now also clearly and greatly agitated with emotional upset.

After a three-count moment, the implications of his answer sank into my mind with devastating effect…but my panic dispersed as I confronted a new critical task.

"I have to get the camera. You go on and finish your climb and get to the top," I called out.

The distance down looked immense, but it probably only took about fifteen minutes to descend the one hundred feet to where the camera pouch lay, wedged between two rocks and looking barely scuffed. I opened the case and examined the piece, which seemed intact. I flipped the "On" switch. No, no, no… it would not come back to life. It was as if my very soul had been stabbed with a sword. Despair overwhelmed me. My only thoughts were that, for me, all was now done there. What good was it to continue? Bright sun and blue skies, but a fatalistic darkness of mind… two hundred feet short of my Namesake Mountain summit.

I soon heard new cheering from above, shrieking and yelling confirming that my son had completed the climb alone and was at the top. I could smile for that. At least he made it. My time would have to be some other day.

"Are you all right, Dad, are you okay?" Justin called down.

"I found the camera, but it's broken…and I'm not coming up," I called back to him. "I'll wait for you here." Justin and Tom rejoined me within about twenty more minutes.

Once they reached my position, they both tried to encourage me to make the last effort of the climb, offering to help me, if need be. But I wanted no further part of the thought. My mind was consumed. Without photographic proof of the achievement, it might too easily fall out of memory, as well as surely invite skepticism from the folks back home. At this stage of my life, fear of being doubted far outweighed any satisfaction of what at that moment appeared an empty accomplishment. I was totally unstrung mentally and felt physically exhausted. I thanked them but declined.

With one last look up at the summit, one last consideration of the choice I was making, I announced, "Let's go back down!"

The three of us then proceeded slowly downward, each step feeling even more precarious than on the way up. Tom took the lead again, but cautioned for us to not follow on a directly vertical line of him and each other. The loosening of rock that often fell away from our footing might hit and injure the person below. It took more than an hour to descend to the rocky plateau which was still steeply sloped at the point we had reached it.

Suddenly, another fit of abdominal pains came over me, and once again I scurried about for a place to relieve my bowels. *Gotta crap again, and this time with no paper!* There were no covering boulders of any kind in sight. I finally squatted, pants down, and nature took its course, the sense of humiliation now overwhelming as I pondered my foul state of being, unsheltered and shamed. Yet another personal misery to be endured this day. Self-loathing now filled my mind. But the earth itself granted one small respite, having directed me unknowingly near a very large patch of green moss in the middle of this wide open and barren, rocky ground. Waddling over just some four meters to it, I was able to more than reasonably clean myself by sliding my posterior on it. The five-foot length of soft moss was soaked with water from a flowing natural spring there. Good grief. A small miracle granted by the mountain gods, indeed!

Tom was far ahead at the edge of the tree line and waited for Justin and me to rejoin him. We still had a considerable way to climb down from there, and some of it was of equal challenge as what we had just completed from the mountain top. As we carefully walked down a ridge full of jumbled large boulders, my legs, weak from the climb, collapsed suddenly, and down I went to my knees. As my two companions looked on with alarm, I smiled and said, "Maybe it's time for a short break."

We took a ten-minute rest, drank the last of the water, and I gingerly flexed and stretched my tired legs. After declaring myself fit and ready again, we set out again and in about thirty minutes, reached the final hiking trail back to camp. Upon reaching the Saddle Ridge, Tom bid us adieu, and I thanked him for his leadership and help getting my son to the top of his mountain. With a wave and call of, "Good luck to you," he continued his way downward, while Justin and I held back to once again rest my very wobbly legs. A view of the sun hovering just above the mountaintops to the west served as timely distraction as I awaited enough leg strength to return.

Walking down the path through the trees, I realized that this day was probably a major defining moment of our father-son relationship and a fork in the road of life. I had, for the second time, reached my breaking point in the presence of Justin, the last on our previous trip to this wilderness, on the Fishfin Ridge that was fully in view. All of my breakdowns sourced directly back to my own failings in preparation, execution of task, and loss of self-composure when dealing with the circumstances I had put us in. My son's triumph this day was heavily overshadowed in my mind by my own failures, and the near future would soon reveal the full impact.

CHAPTER THIRTEEN

Day Fourteen...

Rest and light exertion were the order of this day, the previous three having thoroughly depleted us with physical and mental overload. In addition to sore, weak muscles, we were also quite dehydrated from so much time in the sun and the high altitude. My only urgency this morning was to fill the portable shower water bag to heat it in the sun, hoping to wash away the accumulated sweat, sunscreen, Deet, dirt, and grime of the past four days that had my skin and scalp irritated with crawling itch. Perhaps we would later use the fishing poles on the lake to catch dinner? I had also brought the book about Chief Joseph, so some reading and extra sleep may also fit the need of extra rest.

Breakfast of hot oatmeal and fruit after some coffee was all I accomplished before returning to the tent to read. Of course, that small thing involved walking about one hundred meters of rocky ground to the stream, refilling our purified water supply, walking back, building the fire, boiling that water to cook, and cleaning up after—all after having walked another one hundred meters to the camp toilet facility to deal with the daily constitutional. Justin was also of mind to rest. My reading was modest, a late morning nap overtaking me until about two o'clock that afternoon.

After a quick lunch, the shower water was more than ready, the solar bag having worked faster than I'd hoped. A nearby tree provided a limb just high enough to hang the device, and the longed-for cleansing was accomplished without undue discomfort in the open air and warm sun. The shower device was very efficient, and there was more than enough water left over for my son to share this wilderness camping pleasure, but he declined, preferring to stay in the tent. This pleasure was a solitary experience.

Our next conversation about an hour later was one that I'd put off since long before the beginning of the road trip departure. It involved the issue of my son having taken up smoking tobacco.

It was not good news when his mother had informed me some two months earlier of this discovery. She had not confronted Justin about it since she felt her plate was already full of other disagreements with him. It was up to ol' Dad to give the health talk, just as it had been to belatedly talk about the sexuality issue three years before. Speaking about it in any kind of disapproving manner would've been a hypocritical exercise since I was a smoker hooked on the vice myself, so my conversation with him was more educational about the addictive nature of smoking and the difficulty of quitting. I then semi-demanded he share his hidden smokes since my supply was totally consumed. (Bad Daddy again!) His was a menthol brand, unlike my own. He would no longer have to secretively hide the activity and carry the weight of withholding it from our relationship, which was at best a mixed trade-off.

I later invited him to join me in an attempt to catch a fish dinner from the lake, and he accepted. We proceeded to consume the next couple of hours using the fishing equipment we had hauled out to this wilderness twice. After much hassle, I finally got one of the rod and reel poles to cast with a lure, but after three or four attempts, we went through about another hour of switching to the other lures, and still without success. Finally trying the bait inventory, the recommended one did attract nibbles, as our view of the float confirmed. My second cast was a bit luckier, for the fish took the bait again and I did hook the prey. After reeling him in, he was unfortunately of the size that demanded release, falling well short of the minimal fourteen inches that qualified for harvest.

We managed to unhook him without much trouble and tossed him back. Baiting the hook again, I cast out a bit farther. After some minutes the float began to bob again, and sure enough, ol' Dad was demonstrating long-forgotten skills acquired from his grandfather in days long ago. Hooking a fish for a second time, I pulled him into shore. Out of the water appeared the same damn little guy I had just tossed back. The attempt to unhook him failed due to the hook being completely swallowed, so I had to cut the line to free him. "Fishy" did not survive the ordeal that time, as we soon observed him surface, floating dead in the water.

By the time I had tied a new hook on the line, I was feeling a bit weak from even these light exertions in the late afternoon sun. The wind was down, the shadows of the trees beginning to shade the area, and the mountain mosquitoes were appearing more frequently. Justin declined to give the activity another go, so we declared the fishing complete and headed back to the tent for a second rest before dinner prep would begin.

About an hour later, we rose and prepared our last dinner, which was simple chicken & rice again, and we finished the wine. While the dusk came on and we watched the campfire after our clean-up chores, Justin took a walk away from the campsite to his self-designated tree to urinate. On return, he reported large, strange claw marks in the dirt beside the tree. With flashlight in hand, I accompanied him back to the spot, and though it did look like some kind of disruption may have occurred, my eyes could not discern with any clarity the size of the claws that might have made the marks he was seeing.

With that bit of drama, we returned to the fire for a few more minutes, then dowsed it and entered the tent for the night. I located the pistol and put it within easy reach, but fatigue overcame us quickly after a game of chess, and we slept undisturbed until dawn the next day.

Day Fifteen…

Up early at first light, Justin and I were both feeling "done" with the camping, even though we would be within wilderness for most of the remains of this day. Breakfast was oatmeal and sandwiches while we finished off the milk and made second sandwiches for a lunch, either before or during passage on the trail back to the outfitter camp. Breaking down our campsite went quickly enough that we also had ample time to move all the gear back to the exact spot, some fifty meters away, that it had been dropped off four days prior. It was by then a few minutes after eleven o'clock, so we had a bit of time to kill. For the next hour, we took greater inventory of our surroundings, including rechecking Justin's claw marks in the full light of day. They were still not particularly clear to my eye, but seemed small and might have been a coyote, badger, beaver, wolf, wolverine, or small wildcat of some kind, perhaps marking its turf.

At noon, we decided to eat our lunches, which took less than fifteen minutes, and then we sat around smoking all but one last cigarette for each of us from Justin's remaining stash. Concerns were beginning to weigh on our minds about the lateness of the day, when suddenly Robert appeared with our rides "outta there." The gear loading went smoothly and quickly after Robert took less than five minutes to eat his own lunch. Then he announced a change of plan and began unsaddling his big riding mule. Our guide pointed out that Justin's horse was missing a saddle pad and he began removing her saddle. He quickly re-saddled the horse with the pad from his own ride, and packed his saddle on one of the packhorses that he asserted was carrying the least weight.

Justin and I mounted up, taking one packhorse each in tow as Robert headed off on foot across the campground to the trail, leading by the reigns his own now bareback mount. Once reaching the descending portion of the path, Justin and I stayed mounted since we now were pulling the packhorses, and the ride soon degenerated to real discomfort. We reached the lowest elevation of the path, some eight-hundred feet down, in not much more than an hour. After a short break, our guide led off on foot with his mule up the next ridge. We followed, up the rising trail and the ride comfort did much improve. Robert demonstrated amazing stamina and leg strength, taking only three more breaks during our ascent up and over a good four miles to the outfitter camp. He even found the missing saddle pad halfway up the trail. The eleven-mile transit back had taken just over three and a half hours, and we arrived just past 4:30 P.M. Our trail guide was a very tough and rugged young man of amazing endurance.

Without a word, Robert disappeared as the managing outfitter greeted us with the repaired truck tire and to settle up on the service charges. It turned out that my estimate was the correct one regarding the guide and horse charges, and the tire repair charge was more than fair. I gladly paid, but was surprised when the man then also disappeared into a tent after thanking us for doing business with them, leaving us to our own devices. The repaired tire still required changing, the sun was low, and somehow, I was disappointed by the absence of offers to assist with the chore. Nevertheless, that was to be the way it would be, so my son and I put ourselves to the task. Having done it before, we completed the deed in about twenty minutes. We then reloaded our gear back into the truck, including the forgotten lawn chairs that were near the corral area, set next to a tree.

I was agitated with the end service, tired, and irritated with Justin's lethargic movements as we dealt with the gear loading and tire change. I once again started criticizing his performance as we slowly began driving out of the trailhead. Justin suddenly exploded at me in protest for the first time since he'd been three years of age. He was so mad and fed up that he said he wanted to "kick my ass," and claimed he'd never wanted to come on the trip in the first place. I had greatly wanted Justin to be tough enough to handle himself against school and neighborhood bullies, and had all but insisted on his taking martial arts training. He probably could've "kicked my ass" if he'd had had a real mind to.

I had always felt and spoke of myself as being fortunate over the years concerning my relationship with my son, the complaints of woe from other parents reemphasizing to my mind a sense of true luck. But now I knew that I'd gone more than one rant too far on this trip. Relationship with Justin was the one I valued most, so I was quick to admit being in error. I then authentically spoke of my love for him, admiration of his accomplishments, and respect for his standing up for himself. My questions that followed were, "Why did you come if you truly had not wanted to? What changed? Why hadn't you spoken up sooner?" He'd committed nearly $600 of his own money to this venture, after all.

There was a girl of real interest back home named Kristen.

After a couple of years of prodding our son to reveal any seriously affectionate female interests and drawing blanks, the day had finally arrived. Though he had made slight mention of a girl during our conversations while en-route, his shy nature hadn't revealed anything in particular that might designate her as being possibly "the one." I'd even asked him if he wanted to send her a post card when we were at the Wall Drug, but his response had been that he didn't have her address, or anyone else's.

Lord Baden-Powell may have anticipated a feminist issue when he wrote, "...*Without manliness and good citizenship we are bound to fail. Manliness can only be taught by men, and not by those who are half men, half old women.*"

Scouting taught "chivalry," and recommended that "*when walking with a lady or a child, a scout should always have her on his left side, so that his right is free to protect her.*" Also, when "*meeting a woman or a child, a man should, as a matter of course, always make way for her,*" *even if he has to step off the pavement into the mud."*

Baden-Powell had three rules for romantic relations:

"Don't lark about with a girl whom you would not like your mother or sister to see you with."

"Don't make love to any girl unless you mean to marry her."

"Don't marry a girl unless you are in a position to support her, and to support some children."[21]

The "Teenage Wars" were some of the very worst years with my own father. They drove us to a distant relationship for well over a decade following. I had no intention, if humanly possible, to allow the relationship with my own son to spiral down anywhere near those depths. Admitting my error seemed to provide a much-needed fix of this unexpected relationship breakdown. Besides, we had other concerns as we drove down the mountain road of past woe. The sun was sinking fast and we were *behind schedule again*. Our initial speed was painfully slow, and a deadline that the motel had stipulated for our room reservation back in the town of Salmon loomed large. Go, little Ranger, go!

I pushed the speed as fast as I dared down tilted, loose-gravel surfaces, next to sheer mountain cliffs, hairpin turns, over the ruts and holes, and the ever-present sharp-as-razor-blade rocks. It was after five o'clock when we had started out, and we really, really were looking forward to those motel luxuries we had come to miss. As the road improved, so did our speed, and the sun was low in the sky by the time we pulled up to the motel's office. The Ranger's clock read 7:58 P.M. as I knocked on the already-closed door. The motel manager opened the door at 7:59 with a look of surprise.

"We're here, the McGuire reservation has arrived!" I announced with much relief and satisfaction that we were on time with the motel check-in policy.

After a few moments of hesitation, the manager said, with a stern, serious face that we were too late and would have to look elsewhere for a room. He had already rented out our reserved room and the property was now fully occupied. I countered that he himself had informed me that the policy was eight o'clock P.M. before such a thing could happen, and showed him my wristwatch. Before he could assert that my time was wrong, I also pointed at

21 Drewery

his own office wall clock reading 7:56.

At that he lost his demeanor of authority, a slight hint of confusion overtaking him as he fumbled with several pieces of motel paperwork in hand.

I continued by asking, "That is the clock you rely on when documenting reservations and arrival times, isn't it?"

My last point was game, set, and match. The man then cooperatively found a set of the room keys, and after hesitating with another thought in frozen posture, he said, "Yes, this will be okay." He handed over the keys with the words, "Sorry about the confusion. Enjoy your stay."

I accepted the keys and we made our way to the room, by happy happenstance its location not requiring us to move our vehicle. Unpacking quickly, we put off showers as we opted instead to eat dinner at the coffee shop before it closed. Within the hour, we walked back to our room as dusk was in most beautiful display, transforming the clouds in the sky to bright pink and orange, outlined by velvet. Hot showers, soft double beds, and sleep followed in short order after yet another extraordinary day.

The sound of someone loudly entering our room and the shock of bright lights awoke us both with a start and confusion. A voice loudly asked, "What are you doing in our room? This is our room and I have the keys. You two have to move out."

As my eyes opened and focused, two large guys in rough dress holding duffle bags and other gear were standing over us, looking nearly as confused as I, and more than a little upset. It was two o'clock in the morning.

"I have keys, too," I answered as I reached over to the nightstand and dangled them for easy visual confirmation. "I reserved a room here last April, and this is the room and key that the manager gave me."

The intruders began to shuffle their feet, moving back and forth as they processed my information into what was then a real quandary for their circumstance. I offered for Justin and me to share one bed so they could have space to rest, but the men declined and declared their intention to move on and cause no further interruption. With that concession, they quickly departed, leaving the room to us, and we soon were continuing our restful slumber until morning.

Day Sixteen...

Civilization and its magnificent comforts after the rigors of wilderness living cannot be overstressed. The distinctions of scarcity, abundance, leisure, convenience, the ease of mobility, and even having choices in the matter become very powerful and clear. It is also the place where there are a lot more people around to provide goods, services, and diversity of conversation, all which can be sorely missed.

Justin and I chose to sleep in a bit later, rousing ourselves around eight in the morning. Breakfast back at the coffee shop and planning for the day was complete by 9:30 A.M., and the tasks began from there. Laundry again was dropped off, and then we revisited the local photography shop to see if my camera could be salvaged, or at least the film locked within. The shop's owner was present and took the camera back to his darkroom to investigate our problem. Reappearing within a few minutes, he declared the camera dead for good, but he was able to salvage the film. Though he advertised film development services, he made clear that it couldn't be finished before our departure, so I added the roll rescued to the three others I had completed. The owner then offered to buy my broken camera for $10 to use as parts in lieu of a cash fee, which I in gullible ignorance accepted too quickly, and off my son and I went to investigate more of the town.

Walking down the main street, we looked in on some of the shops that sold clothing, outfitting gear, novelties, and real estate, as well as some of the other restaurants, eateries, bars, and entertainment clubs. We walked in the warmth of the sun from shop to shop, and finally chose one for lunch that satisfied our renewed afternoon appetites. The laundry was ready later, and after picking it up, we opted for eating in the room that night, taking advantage of the kitchenette feature of our accommodation. Next was the grocery, where ingredients for a pork chop dinner with all the trimmings was secured before returning to the motel for an afternoon nap.

At about six o'clock we awoke and prepared to go back to the pizza parlor where the rafting guides would be conducting their end-of-voyage group party. I gathered the rocks from the top of our mountain, which I had promised to each of our guides. The stones were actually no larger than medium-sized gravel rock, but we had brought back a bunch and we were eager to share the victory. We still harbored a great fondness for the folks on our rafting guide team, and their camaraderie that was a big "missing" from our own past week of adventure.

Within the next hour, we drove over to the location and quietly approached Susan and Natalie, who were closest to the door of our entrance. They were engaged in conversation with a couple of folks from their last run of the river, and it was a few moments before they noticed our presence. After at first a quizzical look, sudden excited smiles and exclamations poured forth as our beaming smiles of mutual recognition mirrored each other. Susan's eyes were dancing as she asked The Question: "Did you guys make it? Did you make it to the top of the mountain?" Natalie looked on with equal anticipation.

"Justin made it, and I got close enough," I acknowledged, and both girls let out a "Whoop!" and prolonged, "Yeah!"

They then each hugged Justin with passionate approval and yelled out to the other guides that we were back, returned from the mountain. When presenting each woman a rock from the top, their expressed gratitude well matching the symbolic value my son and I attached to the gesture. Locating our three other beloved guides present within the crowd, a duplicate presentation of those promised little rocks was made, that the rock might serve to remind of a story to be told.

Our visit was not long, lasting little more than the consumption of a beer, but it was a real highpoint. One interesting tid-bit of news from Matt was that the group had seen a mountain lion chasing a deer near the shore line on this most recent trip. But soon, Justin and I ended our visit since it was we who were the intruders on this evening, crashing a party meant to be in honor of others. We took our leave after last farewells, and then returned directly to the motel to begin our own dinner and last night of relaxation. I dove right into the cooking, and Justin located an HBO movie that we enjoyed on the TV as we ate. We retired for the night well satisfied. Our Road Trip would resume at first light of the morrow.

CHAPTER
FOURTEEN

Day Seventeen…

Departure was by seven o'clock in the morning, and our Ranger was soon climbing up through the forest to the Lost Trail Pass at the Continental Divide, then onward into Montana and the downslope of the Bitterroot Mountain Range. Justin had dozed back to sleep as we retraced the road through this state, the beauty of which was left for my eyes alone to enjoy. We had both been quiet in conversation, and my teen son did require more sleep for his still-maturing body, so there was a reduced sense of any problems. During the shopping for dinner the previous day, some snacks and fruit had also been procured, and these served as a light brunch as the miles clicked by.

The time was around two o'clock when we drew close to the Little Bighorn Battlefield National Monument, and I declared that I wanted to take this opportunity to see it. My brother, Rob, had visited the site some years previously, and had spoken glowingly of it being well worthwhile. There were a number of cars in line awaiting entrance, but soon we were paying the modest admission fee. We pulled in and bypassed the parking area—the map indicated a continuation of the roadway that connected two of the three major conflict points of the battle and would pass by for viewing most of everything between.

As our vehicle traversed the pavement that snaked along the buttes above the Little Bighorn River valley, the size and scope of this violent clash became quickly apparent. Most folks know the place as Custer's Last Stand, but the actual battle was far more complex and interesting, as can easily be understood when viewing the battleground. It encompasses nearly four to five miles of the moving skirmish, battle, siege, and massacre of the men fighting with the general himself. Over half of the soldiers of the 7th Cavalry Regiment did survive, and the years since have provided people a wealth of literature about the event. In addition, Hollywood has found the tale compelling enough to create multiple movies that intrigue Americans today as much as the battle did in the direct aftermath.

Justin and I started our self-guided tour by moving to the south end of the park, where a vantage point allowed view of where the engagement began. Preset viewing scopes sighted the spots of terrain that the posted explanations referred to. Since the ground is wide open and little changed since 1876, the observer easily visualizes the firefight as it unfolded. The sun was as high and warm as it was on the day of the battle, which added realism and context to several aspects of the story.

This particular portion of the battleground was where those who survived had retreated and held out for two days, awaiting either Custer or other relief columns to provide their rescue. The Monument Battleground Park is also an archeological site, such that only sanctioned researchers are usually allowed to step beyond clearly marked pavement walkways, to search out artifacts and clues to the battle. Other small signs warning of rattlesnakes lurking in the tall grasses add more than a little incentive to comply.

It is a one-of-a-kind battleground site because the soldiers who died there were mostly buried where found, and the area is little populated and notably undisturbed. Each original burial spot is now marked with a standard white cross visible from the road and pathways.

George Armstrong Custer had already split his command into three dispersed detachments before he arrived at the battleground. Nearly half of the regiment was still trailing far behind. Splitting his force further, he directed Major Reno, his second in command, to surprise the southern portion of the Native American encampment on the Little Bighorn River. Custer took the remainder of the regiment about three miles north along the top of a large butte formation above and east of the river. He intended to attack the opposite end of the village. His greatest fear throughout the entire expedition had been that the Indians would scatter and run, escaping the wrath that he intended to inflict, as had occurred many times before. Consequently, he proceeded to commit a number of tactical errors that would spell doom for his mission and the men that rode with him.

As Justin and I took in the battleground, the most poignant and telling was the graveyard aspect, of white crosses scattered about the park. It is a stunning panorama for the viewer. Some say it is haunting.

Historians are divided on many details of the battle. But most agree that the cavalrymen and their horses were already nearly exhausted after some thirty-six hours of forced marching to this spot in Montana. As one drives along the path of Custer's last ride, more tightly clustered crosses are the evidence of one group of tired men and horses after another being assigned their portion of his battle plan and left behind their charging leader. With archeological evidence, along with a military and timing analysis of the battle, the most recent assertion is that the command was deliberately spread out in these positions as tactical battle formations. Custer was a very experienced, successful, and famous general in the recent American Civil War as well as prior Indian battles. Regardless, there were a great many more Indians than Custer expected to encounter and the warriors were unusually aggressive. Hostiles closing in from all sides isolated and then overwhelmed the small groups, forcing most of them to fight their individual "last stands."

We eventually moved to Last Stand Hill, where a stirring and glorious stone monument designates where Custer and his remnant cavalrymen of the running fight were overwhelmed. There, a denser group of the white marker crosses lead up to the top, covering about half of an acre. The monument is filled with the names of the soldiers and civilians who died in the battle, including a civilian newspaper reporter named Kellogg. Other scattered markers commemorate some of the Indians who also died in the battle. The fight result was lopsided in favor of the Native Americans. As victors, they carried away most of their fallen tribesmen, so there are not very many Indian markers to be seen.

We then moved on to the museum where an excellent display of artifacts, including weapons, equipment, clothing, photos, and paintings were accompanied by storylines and biographies of the central characters. Though the Native Americans were destined to ultimately find their way to reservation life, the year 1876-77 would confirm that these people would not surrender quietly.

The beauty and majesty of these still nearly pristine places leaves little doubt as to why the Native Americans resisted with such passion the encroachments of the white peoples from the east. The Great Plains Indian Horse Culture was coming under final assault, along with the freedoms of that way of life. Western cultural progress soon snuffed it out of existence, as it did the great buffalo herds, for economic gain or sport.

The long racial war of genocide that the first European migrations to the Western Hemisphere had ignited against the indigenous populations, were conducted very much due to the greed for gold. This greed had been exhibited from the very beginning by Christopher Columbus, at the very first meeting with indigenous peoples. The conquistadores who followed him were even more rapacious. The Black Hills Gold Rush of the 1870s, after all, was undeniably a trespass by thousands of white gold-seekers on Indian Treaty Lands. The official U.S. government treaty, belatedly offered to the Native Americans for purchase of the Black Hills, was rejected and is still disputed by the Sioux and other Native American tribes to this day.

On completion of the museum, it was decided to skip touring the National Cemetery, also located here, since hunger pangs needing attention. My son had exhibited more interest in this tourist stop and I didn't want to press my luck. We left the park and stopped at a small highway plaza near the Interstate entrance. The lunch of plain, stale sandwiches and lukewarm canned soda were a disappointment, but road food is always an iffy proposition. It did satisfy the issue at hand.

The time was well past four in the afternoon, so the vehicle was fueled and cruising on the road again, continuing homeward through northeast Wyoming. Neither of us were interested in another campout, so we bypassed the Devil's Tower opportunity. With darkness fully upon us, we decided to skip the Rapid City motels also, since our energy still felt strong, and drove for another couple of hours until the black and sparsely traveled road had sapped my last. We pulled into a highway rest area to doze until the next daylight.

Day Eighteen...

The morning sun was breaking the horizon when we awoke, and our vehicle was underway quickly. We were already halfway through South Dakota and almost immediately crossed over the Missouri River. It was about an hour later that we were approaching the spot of our first breakdown of the previous year. That was where a kind and helpful farmer had been of great contribution to us while in need.

Pulling off at the exit and turned into his drive, Justin and I both walked up and gave a knock on his door. Fortune was with us as Karl was there and answered. After a bit of a bewilderment at our appearance, recognition slowly transformed his face into a broad smile when we explained who we were, and what had happened since he had helped us that fateful evening of our past meeting.

With renewed thanks, I presented one of the larger rocks, expressing our wish that he accepted it as a memento of our appreciation. He seemed quite taken with the explanation that we had found and conquered the mountain and that the rock was from the top. I further shared our hopes that this memento would suffice as proof for a story he might later tell…a story of two strangers broken down on the highway who arrived at his door, and what goodness of heart can help make possible to the occasional pilgrim who happens by. With that, Karl took the rock and thanked us. Wishing the best for him and his family, we then took our leave back to the red Ranger and pulled back onto the highway.

By the time we reached Sioux Falls, we were ready to eat. We'd also decided to take a different route home that might prove a bit faster, as well as provide a different landscape to occupy the hours. After lunch at a national-chain family restaurant, we continued west into Minnesota, but the Great Plains' flatness and the arrow-straight highway didn't change a wit. If anything, the landscape flattened more so, was practically treeless, and the roadway became laser-straight to the horizon ahead. The only variance was that of the occasional, artificial small hill of an overpass. It was one field of grain for as far as the eyes could see for miles and miles. The mundane topography finally morphed back into familiar, rolling farm country as we neared the Mississippi River and the city of La Crosse, Wisconsin, on the other side. The fourth crossing of this mighty waterway was finally a day-light experience, but the Interstate bridge construction work did little for the view.

Traffic had been steadily increasing since an hour before crossing the state line, and by the time we were near Madison, Wisconsin, metro area, the driving required more careful awareness. There are many descriptions of drivers in this country, and most folks have little confusion when those descriptions are applied. There is the aggressive driver, the defensive driver, the careless driver, etc., with quite a few subsets and combinations. Our vehicle was piloted by what may've been coined a long-destination driver: cruising as close to the limits as possible, behaving with the proper etiquette of advanced signaling, maintaining proper distance, and generally being as predictable to others as possible. Time would take care of itself, and we just wanted to get to our destination in one piece.

While maintaining this responsible driving pattern, a slower and erratically moving sedan we were attempting to pass suddenly lurched over into the passing lane we were occupying, nearly colliding with our vehicle. I braked and pulled over farther to the left, avoiding contact, and blaring the horn. The man in the sedan straightened back into his proper lane while pulling quickly ahead and away.

Is this guy drunk or something? Fine! It's okay to just follow, I thought, settling back to the cruising speed. But, within three or four miles, we were catching up to the sedan, which was once again slowing and swerving.

"He must be drunk! Need to get by and away from this guy."

I then floored the accelerator and succeeded in passing the car. But, oh, what a sight! We spied a young woman suddenly pop up and appear wearing a big grin, matching her companion's, and they both looked back at us in the exact moment our vehicles were side-by-side. He held up a beer can as a toasting gesture, took a drink, then passing the can to the woman. Wisconsin does have a reputation of possessing six out of the top ten alcohol consuming town populations in the country. Madison is a college town. More temptations for my son on the figurative horizon, I'm thinking. Or was something else more risqué going on? We both spontaneously started laughing from the scene just observed.

"Justin, there are many kinds of distracted driving, and all are just as dangerous as drinking. Please refrain from crazy stuff like that, ok?"

"Gotcha there, Dad."

After this quasi-comic relief, the balance of the journey was uneventful, except for a renewed chill in the relationship with Justin. He had been mostly silent on this Road Trip, neither sharing his thoughts nor responding to my own topics of discussion since the beginning. It was like trying to converse with a secret agent. In retrospect, it's clear that my conversation of disappointments during much of the last two days did little to improve the matter. I'd said little to assuage the pains of his own insecurities and disappointments. He no doubt harbored resentments of my criticisms of his music and driving. I was tired and crabby, and perhaps a distasteful kind of company to be with.

At one point my exasperation with him reached the point where I blurted out, "Maybe this should be our last trip together for a while, since you don't seem to enjoy them very much."

"That's fine with me," he answered with brevity, and a good hour elapsed before any conversation resumed.

Once approaching the outskirts of our hometown, both mood and comments turned more positive when reviewing the highpoints of the adventure. Much had been accomplished. There were achievements to be quite proud of.

As a team, we had traversed both road trips intact physically and with minimal loss. Points of interest including the Badlands, Devil's Tower, the Indian battlegrounds, and a 100-mile whitewater rafting journey through the wilderness, which were all laudable sights and amazing activities to engage in. Riding horseback with real cowboys on the mountain trails was a new thrill. Vehicle troubles had been overcome. And, we had found better ways of accomplishing our objectives each trip.

The Namesake Mountain had been found, its surroundings hiked and explored, the eminence climbed twice, and photographed in detail. The total ascending direct climb distance was over 1,430 feet up, into thin air above the 8,650-foot starting point. With the additional preliminary 200+ foot ridge to be climbed each way, the true round-trip climb was nearly 2,000 feet, with over half considered a rock scramble, requiring more than occasional use of all four limbs in ground and rock contact. Mount McGuire is considered a Class 2 mountain climb. Our efforts exceeded climbing both the Empire State Building and the World Trade Center on consecutive days. And one need not crawl the last 1,000 feet, like on our mountain! Including the prior year backpacking, our ascending climb total was over a mile into the sky! Seeing up-close-and-personal a beauty and majesty most people never would, Justin had accomplished nearly every goal we had set out for ourselves. He had reached the summit on his own! In detail, I shared my acknowledgements of him, my pride, and admiration.

"So, what was your favorite part of the trip, Justin?"

"Getting to the top, of course."

"What was your least favorite part of the trip, aside from my displeasure with your music and driving?" I chuckled.

"Well, those are definitely up on the list," he offered with his own laugh. "But mostly it was not having you at the top of Mount McGuire with me."

"Yeah, me too. Maybe someday," was all I could offer in response.

At his Mom's house, he safe, sound, and home before midnight, we exchanged heartfelt hugs of mutual affection.

"See ya at work, Dad." he called back to me from the doorstep, and into the house my boy disappeared.

CONCLUSION

Wilderness, defined, is a tract of land or region uncultivated and uninhabited by human beings. The landscape is essentially undisturbed by human activity together with its naturally developed life community. A wilderness might be a large, empty, or pathless area, or even part of a garden devoted to wild growth. Another use of the word may regard a personal state of mind, as in a bewildering situation, or being bewildered. My great fear was that yet another endeavor I had undertaken had blown up in my face. The Dad is now confronted with the realization that his boy is gone, replaced by an independent-minded young man. Justin had come to full realization that his father is just another flawed adult, and not always the good guy with good news. My illusion of partnership, as I'd contrived it, had been devastated.

Clearly, Justin and I had reached a fork in the road of life. I was bewildered. A new paradigm had come into existence. My son would choose a path asserting his own mind more forcefully, and his decisions and choices henceforth would not always seek my council nor agreement. My consent was no longer a necessary factor. A powerful masculinity had come to the fore within him. The final line of demarcation from his childhood was crossed as his transformation into becoming a man had occurred before my eyes. Much like learning to swim, that extinguishes a fear of deep water, or by personally distinguishing balance, that makes riding a bicycle possible, his boundaries in life were now exponentially expanded. He was no longer the junior partner of our relationship.

When Justin and I returned from this second vacation adventure, sympathetic ears listened with great interest, and communications were most congratulatory. The new photographs were once again spectacular and enjoyed by all, but the narratives were soon jocularly edited by my brothers, to ensure my son was the hero of the tale. In truth, this new narrative, created in a bit of jest, is not so implausible an interpretation. In fact, it was better than my own.

Though Justin was the so-called "junior partner" of the excursions, it was he who had said, "Let's go for it," when

HondaCar became very iffy transport.

It was he who announced, "We're doing this," when I declared we stop, practically at the beginning of the backpacking hike.

And it was Justin who asserted, "Yes, I can," on the climb, pushing forward and conquering the Namesake Mountain summit.

We had faced the toil and fears of terrain and predators, heard whispers of spirits or gods, and survived the cold, snow, and rain. Against many odds, we had climbed a mountain with our name on it, without falling off. What made the experience uniquely powerful was the context of our success. That context, for me, was a new clarity of who I was being as a father, a dad, and as a person. The biggest personal transformation for myself was a discernible sense of confidence and confirmation that I didn't suck as a parent. Gone were the suspicions and feelings of falling short, of being just the substitute and part-timer.

What my siblings had orchestrated in their re-interpretation of my accounts crystalized the real purpose I had been blindly pursuing all along. I could finally see what the real commitment was all about. It was not really just about me and my own criteria of personal accomplishment. The real commitment of the endeavor, the real heart of the matter, was the intention for my son to thrive. And he did, in most unpredictable, astonishing, and admirable ways in the next few years.

The following months witnessed a new status quo, but our relationship did retain warmth as my son and I worked together, shared meals at the all-night diner afterwards, and kept up with each other's doings and news. There were dramas to be shared about his mother, concerns for his senior year academic performance, the college choice, and his preparedness for that new endeavor. A gradual reduction of these meet-ups occurred as time moved on into the next year. In the spring of 1998, I changed employers, and our get-togethers became even more infrequent. Justin continued his job through the end of the summer, and then moved on, leaving the city for college in the fall.

Life sometimes deals surprises, occasionally hard ones. Such occurred in October when we heard word that Justin's Tae-Kwan-Do friend, Jimmy W., had died suddenly, at just 18 years of age. Jimmy had been a good friend of my son, and his passing was a blow of nearly equal sadness to all who had known him, myself included. I attended the funeral. Justin, as well as Debbie and Ken, who knew Jimmy very well, were there, and that did serve as a bit of silver lining to the affair. It had been about three months since I'd seen and talked with my son. Accompanying Justin was a young lass who was introduced as his new girlfriend, Sue. They had attended the same grade in primary and high schools, were now reacquainted at college, happily dating, and building a relationship that appeared of a more serious nature. Debbie was quite tickled by the prospect.

The next month, at the McGuire Family Thanksgiving gathering, Justin asked me the advisability of announcing his plans for getting married to his young lass. He declared he still intended to continue with college even though she had dropped out, but their love was true and that she was "The One!" Since Sue was not present, at her own family's gathering and not ours, I cautioned that he should probably hold off until she included herself at the Christmas gathering.

When Christmas arrived, Justin reported two more hard, personal blows. His sweetheart, Sue, had proved false to their love, and they were no more. Of at least equal upset was that his college course performance had proved insufficient to remain in the school. Later discussion with him revealed that his class attendance had been sabotaged by too many late-night outings to a coffee shop, drinking too much caffeine, engaging in world problem solving chatter with Sue and a few other late-night indulging students of the school. Many morning classes were missed. But one of the regular coffee-crowd participants, likewise engaged, was a guy named Ryan, a very special new friend, indeed.

Ryan was also a freshman student, the same age as my son, and from our home town. He had attended different schools than Justin, but was to become the most engaging and intimate friend my son had ever known. Not only was this young man smart, articulate, and very glib socially, he was also an inspiration. Ninety-five percent paralyzed, he was quadriplegic and wheelchair bound. Ryan had been born with muscular dystrophy, thus from a very young age he faced life while looking at the doorstep of his own funeral. The life expectancy of boys with this condition normally does not exceed their late teens or early twenties. Yet, with a boundless optimism and personal courage, Ryan had committed himself to live his life full-out, no matter what the duration may be.

Justin successfully rebuilt his life the following spring and summer with a new restaurant job working with is Uncle Rob, and a new discipline to be re-accepted back into the same college for the next fall term. He reintegrated himself back in with his buddies there, including spending more time with his friend, Ryan. The friendship thrived because Justin treated Ryan like "one of the guys." Studies and grades improved while Justin also commuted home on the weekends to work part-time for extra cash. The following school year, Ryan submitted a proposal to my son. Since they were hanging out together so much at school, would Justin consider taking on being Ryan's paid, full-time care giver? Though not a particularly well paid position, Justin accepted.

Being a full-time care giver for the disabled is probably one of the most selfless and heroic jobs on the planet. The description of duties is as follows:

Caregivers work in the home and help their clients with daily activities, such as bathing and bathroom functions, feeding, grooming, taking medication, and some housework. Caregivers help clients make and keep appointments with doctors, provide or arrange transportation and serve as a companion for their clients.

In the case of Ryan, they shared a dorm room and the duties would also include lifting him from bed, dressing and undressing him daily, transporting him to and from his college classes, managing his books and papers, assistance with changing sitting and laying positions in chairs and bed, refilling his beer cup, assisting with and managing electronics and video gaming... Intimacy of the most extraordinary kind, that likely could include escorting his friend to death's door.

Of all the accomplishments and endeavors I'm most proud of my son for, the three years that he served as Ryan's care giver at college, while being a student himself, stands out at the top of the list. Trustworthy, Loyal, Helpful, Friendly, Courteous, Kind, Obedient, Cheerful, Thrifty, Brave, Clean, and a Reverence for the possibility of humanity.

Meriwether Lewis, as he assessed the characteristics of the Shoshone warriors and chiefs in 1805, while trekking along the Salmon River:

"... they are also fond of games of wrisk. they are frank, communicative, fair in dealing, generous with what little they possess, extreemly honest, and by no means beggarly... each individual is his own sovereign master, and acts from the dictates of his own mind; the authority of the Cheif being nothing more than mere admonition supported by the influence which the prop[r]iety of his own examplary conduct may have acquired him in the minds of the individuals who compose the band. the title cheif is not hereditary, ... in fact every man is a cheif, but all are not an equal influence on the minds of other members of the community, and he who happens to enjoy the greatest share of confidence is the principal Chief." [22]

This is who I know my son to be.

22   Bergon

Who really was the person named McGuire, that the mountain is named after? After years of personal investigation, the information uncovered confounds a definitive answer. There are at least two other mountains in North America that complicate the issue. Did we climb the wrong edifice? Yet another potentially interesting inquiry and tale to be told.

The Lion

What of the explanations for the multitude of rocks observed, that looked like giant petroglyphs and sculptures? Again, another question that conventional answers like, "they're just rocks," when compared to the multitude of sites in the Americas with similar physical characteristics, appears preposterous. Naturally formed is an answer that is just unacceptable. So, who, when, how, and why? There has been at least 20,000 years of human habitation of the Western Hemisphere. Little more than 3,000 years of that time has even the sketchiest of detail. The official answers fall way short and often fail credibility.

Where were all the advertised wolves, lions, and bears (Oh my!)? An article in a river rafting adventure magazine soon provided an interesting insight.

Three years prior to our own river rafting voyage, a group similar to ours had encountered a whole pack of bears during their evening camp, about half way through their trip on the Middle Fork Salmon River. Five bears had aggressively harassed the camp all night despite the loud clanging of pots and pans, a large bright fire, shouting, the throwing of rocks and even firebrands at the giant, predatory varmints. Fortunately, one of the guides successfully contacted the forest service, who, with great difficulty, came to the rescue the next morning. So, it seems that during the summer, the lions and bears at least, had moved down into the lower valleys where more plentiful food was located, including "filet of river-rafter."

Would I ever return, to summit Namesake Mountain myself?

Justin on Mt. McGuire, 2003. Dad did buy a new camera

Though my son's conquest of Mount McGuire would prove just a stepping stone into his future, my experience would mirror the metaphoric saying, "Everyone has many mountains to climb in life." Along with an obsession of somehow returning to complete a climb to the top myself, other long-desired allegorical "mountain conquest" were very soon encountered or intervened in the years to follow. On many intimate and most dear frontiers of life including relationships, career, and health, another set of unpredictable road trip adventures and challenges were soon calling with powerful voice.

The following was the dearest and most powerful of all:

I had been a two-time loser at love, and had lost the families created from those loves of my past. This story has been about an adventure with my child of the second family, and my personal pursuit of seeking the dignity of being a father and a Dad. But there had existed a committed relationship and family that preceded this account, by about ten years, and another child, who had disappeared from my life to places unknown.

One morning in early January of 1999, just after my son's disappointing first semester of college, my brother Patrick called me with a question. He asked if a woman named Betty was the grandmother of my daughter. He'd seen her obituary in the morning newspaper. We discussed the probabilities, and on completion of the call, I rushed out to purchase a newspaper of my own to set eyes on the notice. Yes, the survivor names mentioned in the obituary did seem to match, and though my daughter's name was not mentioned, her mother and aunt were. I then called the funeral home to inquire about the time and place of the funeral or memorial service, but found that the services had been performed the preceding week. My request for contact information on the survivors was declined, due to privacy issues.

I then inquired if I might donate to the charitable entity mentioned as Betty's preference, and also have forwarded a memorial letter to all eight of the survivors mentioned in the notice. The woman on the phone said the donation would be appreciably forwarded as well as the memorial letters. I sent a cash donation that very day.

With much heartfelt warmth and no small amount of regret for opportunities of relationships lost, a memorial letter was composed over the next week, and sent. I had always had warm feelings for Betty, but in the very few interactions with her, after her daughter and I had gone our different ways, there was also a deep embarrassment and sense of failure. My life had been quite the mess in those days of two decades past, which was about the same time of my last contact with Betty, and any continuing information about my daughter and her whereabouts.

Over the intervening years, I'd made several sporadic attempts to re-establish contact, but the efforts were not concerted, and had fallen short. A new opportunity had suddenly presented itself. Included, was an extra memorial letter address to my daughter, along with my contact information and offer to be in correspondence.

Whether it would be forwarded to her, and whether or not she would choose to correspond, were not givens. There were many a tale of efforts by others I'd known attempting such actions, both as the estranged parent, and as the child of family separations. Most seemed to be stories of sadness, bitterness, anger, vindictiveness, and a choice made of no further pursuit of contact and relationship. My guiding thought was, "One must do what one can do." Feeling like yet another roll of the dice, my hopes were for the best.

Days and weeks went by, and thoughts moved to other things. My routines of work, socializing, and such, resumed as their usual. Then, on returning home from working late in the evening, close to midnight on Valentine's Day, the blinking red light of my land-line telephone indicating a new message. The voice was of a youthful high pitch, and a halting cadence.

"Hello … This is Melissa … I wanted to call and thank you for the donation you sent for my Grandmother. I'm sure she would have appreciated it very much … I also wanted you to know that I would like to talk to you … You can reach me anytime at this number … Thank you again for honoring my Grandmother … Goodbye."

A new Namesake Mountain of Possibility.

SOURCES

Ambrose, Stephen E. *Undaunted Courage: Meriwether Lewis, Thomas Jefferson and the Opening of the American West.* Touchstone; Simon & Schuster Inc., 1996.

Baden-Powell, Robert. *Scouting for Boys*: *The Original 1908 Edition.* Dover Publications, 2007.

Barnes, Ian. *The Historical Atlas of Native Americans.* Chartwell Books Inc., 2009.

Beal, Merrill D. *"I Will Fight No More Forever"*: *Chief Joseph and the Nez Perce War.* Univ. of Washington Press, 1963.

Berg, A. Scott., *Lindbergh.* G. P. Putnam's Sons, 1998.

Bergon, Frank. *The Journals of Lewis & Clark.* Viking; Penguin, Inc., 1989.

Bergreen, Laurence. *Marco Polo: From Venice to Xanadu.* Knopf Doubleday Publishing Group, 2007.

Burnham, Frederick Russell. *Scouting on Two Continents.* Doubleday, 1926.

Drewery, Mary. *Baden-Powell: The Man Who Lived Twice.* Hodder & Stoughton, 1975.

Fuller, Margaret. *Trails of the Frank Church: River of No Return Wilderness.* Trail Guide Books, Inc., 2006.

Isserman, Maurice. *Continental Divide: A History of American Mountaineering.* W.W. Norton & Company, Inc., 2016.

Jeal, Tim. *Baden-Powell: Founder of the Boy Scouts.* Yale University Press, 2007.

Kemper, Steve. *A Splendid Savage: The Restless Life of Frederick Russell Burnham.* W.W. Norton & Company, 2016.

Knapp, Richard K. *The History of John Reed's Gold Mine.* North Carolina State Historic Sites, Reed Gold Mine, Midland, N.C., 1999.

Lott, Jack. "Chapter 8." *America: The Men and Their Guns That Made Her Great*, edited by Craig Boddington, Peterson Publishing Co., 1981.

Martin, Charles A. *The last Great Ace: The Life of Major Thomas B. McGuire Jr.* Cove Publishing, 1999.

Meyer, David D. Written article "The Constitutional Rights of Non-Custodial Parents." Article was delivered as the 2006 Sidney & Walter Siben Distinguished Professorship Lecture at Hofstra University School of Law, 2006.

Philbrick, Nathaniel. *The Last Stand: Custer, Sitting Bull, and the Battle of the Little Bighorn.* Viking; Penguin Group, 2010.

Wagner, Frederic C. III. *The Strategy of Defeat at the Little Big Horn: A Military and Timing Analysis of the Battle"* McFarland & Company Publishers, 2014.

William, David. *The Georgia Gold Rush: Twenty-Niners, Cherokees, and Gold Fever.* University of South Carolina Press, 1993.

The U.S. National Forest Service
The U.S. National Park Service
The Boy Scouts of America

ACKNOWLEDGEMENTS

The number of people who have contributed to the creation of this book far exceeds time and space to all be mentioned with due justice to the extent of their help with the result. But there are certain individuals who must be singled out. Without their support, encouragement, and specific conversations, this adventure and book would have been just another couple of passing ideas.

First on the list is my wife, Silvana, who tolerated my many faults while being the solid pillar of unconditional love and faith in my effort. Closely following is Justin's mother, Debby, who against many reservations, entrusted me with her son on what might be classified as, yet another "Hair-brained Scheme." And of course, top tier contributors also include my parents and siblings, particularly my Dad, Joseph McGuire, who first planted the seed that I might write well enough.

Special acknowledgement to my sister, Jeanne, youngest of my siblings, who endured growing up with six older brothers. She chose the more genteel passion of Fine Arts instead of Scouting, yet backpacked the Rocky Mountains for multiple days, fifteen years before my own attempt.

The person who is most responsible for transforming my scribbles and scratches into an actual text might be Reji Laberje, with her writing and author programs and mentoring. Completion of her simple five-week class verified that my book was not only possible, but nearly done. Her compatriot, RaeAnne Scargall, who performed the edits, was a huge help in turning the roughage of my word salads into something palatable.

And finally, special thanks must go to Mike Nicloy, who has continued to keep faith with me as my publisher, despite my delays and dawdling work ethic.

The following organizations are also instrumental entities deserving acknowledgement:
Landmark Worldwide
The Boy Scouts of America
The YMCA
Werner Erhard and Associates
Wikipedia

ABOUT THE AUTHOR

David A. McGuire is married, has 2 grown, independent children, and is still in training as a servant of two dogs and four talking parrots. They are benevolent masters who allow part-time writing, and recreation with his wife while living somewhere within the Indiana Territory of 1803 (see page 22)... on most days. Born and having spent the majority of his life there, other locales of residence in years past include Waukesha, Wisconsin; Tampa, Florida; Houston, Texas; and Sao Paulo, Brazil. Hobbies and entertainments include reading of and traveling to historic places of interest, and storytelling; aside from arguing with his parrots, and people he does not know on the internet.

www.ingramcontent.com/pod-product-compliance
Lightning Source LLC
Chambersburg PA
CBHW071336090426
42738CB00012B/2915